Enchanted Plants

A Treasury of Botanical Folklore & Magic

Varla A. Ventura

NEW PAGE

This edition first published in 2025 by New Page Books,
an imprint of Red Wheel/Weiser, LLC

With offices at:

65 Parker Street, Suite 7
Newburyport, MA 01950
www.redwheelweiser.com

ISBN: 978-1-57863-860-4

Library of Congress Cataloging-in-Publication Data available upon request.

Cover and interior design by Brittany Craig

Images by Angela in the Fields via Creative Market,
Vintage Fair Clip Art by Digital Xpress via Creative Market,
and by Sky Peck Design

Typeset in Arno Pro

Printed in China

WM

10 9 8 7 6 5 4 3 2 1

This book contains information related to plants and is for informational purposes only.
Some of the plants discussed in this book are poisonous and can be lethal if mishandled or
ingested in sufficient quantities. Extreme caution is advised in their handling and use.
Readers using the information in this book do so entirely at their own risk, and the author
and publisher accept no liability if adverse effects are caused.

To Elizabeth Jens,
the most beautiful flower
of them all

Contents

CHAPTER ONE

The Apple Doesn't Fall Too Far, 3

A Queen's Garden of Cultivars and Edible Delights

CHAPTER TWO

The Cottage Garden of Earthly Delights, 55

Humble Foods in Story and Legend

CHAPTER THREE

The Witch's Garden, 91

What Doesn't Kill You Makes Your Heart Grow Stronger

CHAPTER 4

Among the Fields and Valleys, 135

Wildflowers, Meadowlands, and Other Things to Gather

CHAPTER 5

The Woods Are Lovely, Dark, and Deep, 175

Trees, Shrubs, and Woodland Dwellers

CHAPTER 6
The Marsh King's Daughter, 227

Plants That Grow Near Streams, Bogs, Lakes, and the Sea

A WORD OF CAUTION

This book contains plants both mysterious and deadly. Much like the Kingdom of the Fae, the Plant Kingdom is not something to be trifled with. Plants can bring us love, luck, and beauty but they can just as swiftly bring us harm. Pay attention to how you handle any plant but in particular those of the Witch's Garden. There is a reason spells were cast to protect these plants from the hands of foolish mortals, and to protect foolish mortals from these plants. Remember to revere these botanical treasures, and, for Heaven's sake, don't put them in your tea.

From the Desk of Varla Ventura

For as long as I can remember, I have been able to hear plants. If that sounds like a strange sentence to read, it's because it was a strange one to write. It isn't the same way you talk with another person. It's a conversation suspended somewhere between audible and inaudible. It exists in a space that is undefinable, between the tangible and the intangible. Like a fairy tale.

Plants play a significant role in the majority of fairy tales, even if that role is setting the scene. Sleeping Beauty is not nearly as unattainable, or protected, without the thorny brambles that surround her castle during the one-hundred-year sleep. The wild hedge, tangled with the bleached bones and gilded swords of those who tried to rescue the legendary princess, becomes a central part of the conflict of the story. The Grimms' Juniper Tree becomes a character itself, guarding the secrets of filicide beneath its roots. Fairies dwell among the roses and the woods, leaping, lurking, ever watchful. The original concept for this book has been years in the making, and so as a result the list of plants, like my own poison garden, continued to grow. At some point (and at the publisher's behest), I had to make some decisions about what to include and what to cut. For any writer this is one of the more difficult tasks, but I looked upon it the way I look at pruning my garden: It is good for the overall health of the plants or, in this case, the book.

This book is not an encyclopedia. It does not cover all plants, all attributes, all stories. It is a curated botanical collection of plants that have spoken to me, and I hope, speak to you. The lore and the magic come from years of research and my own personal experience in working with these plants, both horticulturally and spiritually.

From the baneful bog to the garden gate, join me as we take a romp through the kingdom of plants and explore their stories, legends, and magic. Don't forget your scissors.

CHAPTER 1

The Apple Doesn't Fall Too Far

A Queen's Garden of Cultivars and Edible Delights

APPLE • GRAPE • HYACINTH • LILY • NARCISSUS • POMEGRANATE • ROSE • TULIP

Queen for a Day

There is a secret hiding within the castle walls: the queen's garden does not belong to her. It belongs to the gardener who soap-washes the aphids from her roses. It belongs to the creatures, natural and supernatural, who guard and nourish every plant. Who coax and coddle and snip at just the right moment, to capture the beauty and the bounty. But don't tell the queen that. She prefers you to walk with her in her illusory bubble, her gloved finger tracing the lines of a velvet petal or falling leaf. Yes, the garden is planted, tended, cultivated, in her honor. But does the mortal queen understand that when it comes to the domain of plants, there is a queen who reigns even more supreme? Whether it is Shakespeare's Titania, Celtic Queen Maeve, or the Queen Clarion, the Queen of the Fairies is the true ruler of flower, stem, and leaf.

Walk with me, a little while, among these hedges. We'll stay in the shadows and observe the garden as it grows. We will smell the apple blossoms on the wind. Spill the seeds of the pomegranate like a wound upon the white tablecloth. The plants in this section of the garden I have chosen because they represent a certain royal expectation. They are by no means in every queen's garden, nor are they all exotic. Instead, they are plants that have caught my eye time and time again in fairy tales and folklore, urging me to collect them. I place them in your hands.

Apple

But I am done with apple-picking now.
Essence of winter sleep is on the night,
The scent of apples: I am drowsing off.

—Robert Frost, "After Apple Picking"

Botanical name: *Malus pumila* (see the following)

Native to: Mountains of central Asia

Also called: *Malus pumila* is the most widely accepted botanical name, but it is also referred to as *Malus domestica, Malus sylvestris, Malus communis,* and *Pyrus malus.*

Medicinal properties: Apples contain a variety of phytochemicals that are powerful antioxidants, including quercetin, catechin, phlorizin, and chlorogenic acid. These have been shown to reduce the risk of some cancers, cardiovascular disease, asthma, and diabetes.

Magical properties: Under the domain of Venus, slice an apple in half to reveal the star and share the half with another to make them your lover. Apples are frequently used in love spells. The blossoms of apples have an enchanting fragrance and are common ingredients in herbal baths and concoctions to bring love into your life.

The Lore

When I was a young girl, my family moved from the San Francisco Bay Area to a little parcel of land high up in the California foothills, well beyond the reach of electricity. We took our water from a spring on the property, crept out into the moonlight to use the outhouse, and read our books at night by candlelight and kerosene. The property itself held many magical elements for a curious child: forests, an old mine shaft, a pond with a bubbling spring, and, perhaps best of all, the remains of what was once a pioneer apple orchard. It was not just one kind of apple, either, but rather a selection of varieties. Some of these trees grew tall and thin and dropped their fruit from a great distance. Others, like the Golden Delicious, produced fewer fruits, but they hung low and full on the tree. Of all the hundred-year-old trees, though, my favorite was the one that produced no fruit at all but had silvery branches that had arched down right into the ground again, creating a secret fort in the middle. Here, a child could hide for hours, singing off-key and poking at the spiders.

Few botanical specimens invoke such emotion or have such storied history as the apple. Though they come originally from the mountainous region of central Asia, apple trees are one of the earliest fruit trees domesticated by humans, cultivated to produce edible (and rather delicious) fruit. Cultivated apple trees spread throughout Asia to Europe and were introduced to the Americas by the colonizers. The apple is the downfall of mankind's purity in biblical tales, and it is the disguised poison that puts Snow White to sleep. Apples can be sliced open to reveal a star, long thought a symbol of magic and protection. They are sacred to the goddess Aphrodite and so equated with love and valor. Their nectar, aka cider, has played a critical role in history. In his book *The Botany of Desire*, Michael Pollan describes the significance of apples as libation in early colonial days, when water was not as safe to drink as cider. As Pollan reminds us, apples require grafting to produce the varieties we love to pack in a lunch today (looking at you, Pink Lady!); otherwise, you're left with a sour apple, good mainly for cidering.

While there are literally hundreds of cultivars of apples grown today around the world, two apples appear most commonly in stories. The ruby red apple, too tempting to resist, and the golden apple. Whether this was an apple of solid gold or a Golden Delicious (or possibly even an orange), the stories elevate the apple to its place on the altar of the gods. These golden apples are nearly always three things: delicious, elusive, and packed with some kind of transformative magical power.

The Greek goddess Hera has a sacred apple tree gifted to her from Zeus. The tree grows golden apples that grant the eater immortality, but it's guarded by the Hesperides, nymph-goddesses who are associated with evening and the west. Juno, Hera's Roman counterpart, also has a gifted golden apple tree that is protected by Three Maidens of the West, who dance around it and keep it safe. In James Bald-win's *Old Greek Stories*, those maidens chant these lines from a song:

> But a new tree shall spring from the roots of the old,
>
> And many a blossom its leaves shall unfold,
>
> Cheering, gladdening, with joy maddening,
>
> For its boughs shall be laden with apples of gold.

The Greek heroine Atalanta was the swiftest runner in all the land, having been abandoned in the woods as a baby and raised first by bears and then by hunters. A restless soul, she preferred the single life and so devised a plan: she swore that she would only marry one who could win her in a footrace. To make the challenge even harder, she declared any who attempted to race her and lost would be put to death. Sure that this consequence would dissuade would-be suit-ors, Atalanta soon learned that several men, renowned for their running, decided to boldly take on the challenge. Hippomenes (sometimes called Melanion), a handsome young man known for his own swiftness, was chosen as the judge of the race, a task he gravely accepted. He himself could not believe that men would be so foolish to make such an attempt just for a chance at the bride. That was,

According to the 1885 *The Witches' Dream Book and Fortune Teller* by A. H. Noe, "To dream of apples betokens long life and success, a boy to a woman with child, faithfulness in your sweetheart, and riches by trade."

until he laid eyes on her. For not only was Atalanta fierce, but she was also a great beauty. The time came for the race to begin, and as the race began, Hippomenes found himself falling deeply in love with her, her swiftness making her that much more beautiful. And try as they might, one by one, each suitor dropped from the race, weary and heavy with despair. And tragically, each exhausted suitor was led away, presumably to his own death. But the judge, Hippomenes, could not imagine ever parting from Atalanta, and so he announced he, too, would race Atalanta. Atalanta felt sadness that this lovely young man might soon die, but she rested a bit and took up the race. After a quick plea to Aphrodite, asking that he win for the sake of the love in his heart, Hippomenes was ready.

Aphrodite heard his plea, of course, for she had already been at work on his heart making him fall for the beautiful Atalanta in the first place. And, as all interfering Greek gods must, she snuck beside him and handed him three golden apples, whispering instructions in his ear.

At that, the signal was given, and the race began. Atalanta and Hippomenes were so fast that their feet barely touched the ground. But it wasn't long before Hippomenes began to falter, falling behind Atalanta. It was then that Hippomenes tossed onto the path ahead of them one of the golden apples, just as Aphrodite had instructed him to. Immediately, Atalanta was distracted and stopped to pick it up. Hippomenes ran past her. But just a moment later Atalanta caught up with him. Hippomenes again threw another apple ahead, which again distracted her. She stooped to pick it up but lost no time in taking up the race again, zooming past

Hippomenes. With another quick prayer to Aphrodite, he flung the last golden apple onto the path in front of them. For a moment, it seemed that Atalanta was going to ignore it. But Aphrodite was right there, urging Atalanta to take a closer look at the apple, to pick it up and keep it. Unable to resist, Atalanta did just that. In that half-of-a-moment, Hippomenes passed by Atalanta, reaching the finish line first. And so, they married and ran off into the sunset. But it was not happily ever after for the couple. On the day of their wedding, they failed to give thanks to Aphrodite, and the angry goddess turned them both into lions and harnessed them to her own golden chariot.

There are several versions of a story in which a golden apple tree or an entire orchard of golden apple trees grows to ripeness, only to be devoured by a flock of cruel birds. In Andrew Lang's *The Violet Fairy Book*, the story "The Nine Pea Hens & the Golden Apple" begins:

> *Once upon a time there stood before the palace of an emperor a golden apple tree, which blossomed and bore fruit each night. But every morning the fruit was gone, and the boughs were bare of blossom, without anyone being able to discover who was the thief.*

Likewise, in the turn-of-the-twentieth-century collection *Turkish Fairy Tales and Folk Tales* by Ignácz Kúnos, we find the short story "Boy-Beautiful, the Golden Apples, and the Werewolf" in which a magical apple tree grows for a particularly enthusiastic emperor:

> *The Emperor was wild with joy at the thought that he had in his garden an apple-tree, the like of which was not to be found in the wide world. He used to stand in front of it, and poke his nose into every part of it, and look at it again and again, till his eyes nearly started out of his head. One day he saw this tree bud, blossom, and form its fruit, which began to ripen before him. The Emperor twisted his moustache, and his mouth watered at the thought that the next day he would have a golden apple or two on his table, an unheard-of thing up to that moment since the world began.*

In most versions, the emperor offers rewards to anyone who can catch the apple thief. The thieves are, in fact, a flock of birds—sometimes peahens, cranes, pheasants, or swans—one of which shapeshifts into a beautiful maiden who enchants whoever is guarding the apples. She leaves an apple or two so that he might be seen the hero. The secrets are revealed by a supernatural creature. In Lang's version this "creature" is a witch who scares the birds away. In Kúnos's tale, a helpful werewolf saves the day by giving insider information to the boy in the center of the quest.

The Norse tell stories of the gardens being home to the most delicious golden apples in the world, tended by Idun, the goddess of youth. The other gods come to her for the magical apples, which aid in their immortality. These apples have an unusual flavor, but the Heroes of Asgard love them because they could eat a few bites of one of Idun's apples and find themselves rejuvenated and full of joy and happiness. They were the most requested fruit of the heroes on any journey.

The deep red apple is the other apple that makes an appearance in stories. In the Grimm Brothers' collection, "Snowdrop," which is the original story now commonly known as "Snow White," the evil queen fails to kill Snowdrop with a poison comb so returns to her castle with a new plan:

> She went by herself into her chamber and got ready a poisoned apple: the outside looked very rosy and tempting, but whoever tasted it was sure to die.

The queen then dresses up like an innocent peasant peddling apples, who implores Snowdrop to take one:

> Now the apple was so made up that one side was good, though the other side was poisoned. Then Snowdrop was much tempted to taste, for the apple looked so very nice; and when she saw the old woman eat, she could wait no longer. But she had scarcely put the piece into her mouth when she fell down dead upon the ground.

Also found among the Grimm collections, the somewhat bizarre tale "Mother Holle" features two lazy and ugly stepsisters and one Cinderella-like beauty who is made to do all the housework, including sitting at a spinning wheel spinning yarn until her fingers bleed. The blood drips onto the spindle, and when the poor girl stops to wash it off, the spindle goes flying into the well. Naturally, the cruel stepmother punishes the girl and makes her climb in after it. Turns out, the well is actually a portal into another world where otherwise inanimate objects come to life, specifically food. Bread begs to be taken from the oven, and an apple tree beckons her to harvest.

> "Shake me, shake me, I pray," cried the tree, "My apples, one and all, are ripe."

> So, she shook the tree, and the apples came falling down upon her like rain; but she continued shaking until there was not a single apple left upon it. Then she carefully gathered the apples together in a heap and walked on again.

The apple picking is just one of the tasks the girl must complete in this other world. Her industriousness is rewarded with oodles of gold. Incidentally, the girl's lazy sister tries to go through the portal to also gain riches but ends up being tarred and feathered, as she refuses to do any hard work. She walks right by the magical talking apple tree.

Conversing with trees is not unusual in folklore and fairy tales, and apple trees have long been a source of enchantment and power, as well as a valuable resource for sustenance. Recorded in the written record as early as the mid-16th century, apple howling or apple wassailing was a popular practice in which an apple tree in every orchard was chosen for a form of worship. In their marvelous collection *Treasury of Folklore: Woodlands & Forests*, authors Chainey and Winsham describe wassailing, which usually takes place in late winter or early January, as a ceremony that is divided into five stages: choosing a tree; singing and dancing around the tree; making an offering of cider poured onto the roots of the tree; firing off something to ward off evil spirits (such as guns); and finally, placing an offering of bread, often soaked in cider, within the branches of the tree. Revelers would go from orchard to orchard, bringing in the good luck and prayers for an abundant apple harvest. Sounds like a good time to me!

Bobbing for apples is a Halloween-season custom that is popular in Ireland and Wales as well as other parts of England and Europe. In Wales, it is called *twco am 'falau*. Toss a dozen or so apples into a tub of cold water and let the children try to grab them with their teeth. Another more dangerous variation has an apple on one end of a stick and a burning candle on the other. This contraption is dangled by a string, and the person must try to take a bite without singeing their hair on the candle.

In Irish mythology, golden apples grow on the Silver Branch. The white and silvery branch extends into the Otherworld, or the world of the supernatural and fairy kingdom, as W. Y. Evans-Wentz describes in *The Fairy-Faith in Celtic Countries*:

> To enter the Otherworld before the appointed hour marked by death, a passport was often necessary, and this was usually a silver branch of the sacred apple-tree bearing blossoms, or fruit, which the queen of the Land of the Ever-Living and Ever-Young gives to those mortals whom she wishes for as companions; though sometimes, as we shall see, it was a single apple without its branch. The queen's gifts serve not only as passports, but also as food and drink for mortals who go with her. Often the apple-branch produces music so soothing that mortals who hear it forget all troubles and even cease to grieve for those whom the fairy women take.

It may well be that the "golden apples" of some of these stories are oranges, suggesting that we are, in fact, comparing apples to oranges.

In Northern Ireland, two connected lakes known as Lough Erne or Loch Éirne are the setting for the Irish story "The Golden Apples of Lough Erne" or "The Story of Conn-eda." In his 1888 collection *Fairy and Folk Tales of the Irish Peasantry*, William Butler Yeats includes a story in which Conn-eda is sent on an epic, and seemingly impossible, quest. He must procure three golden apples, a black horse, and a supernatural puppy that lives under the lake, which is the realm of the Firbolg, early Irish settlers who were ultimately overthrown by the Tuatha De Dannan, the fierce supernatural kings and queens of Ireland. But why Conn-eda? His father, the king, has many children, but Conn-eda is his favorite. Though Conn-eda's mother has died, the king's new wife is convinced her son will not receive his just deserts, so she devises the plan: her son and Conn-eda will play chess, and whoever wins must go and get the apples. Alas, Conn-eda loses. But because he is kind and fearless and undaunted by the request, he is aided along the way by a powerful Druid and is ultimately successful in getting the apples. He plants the three golden apples in his garden, and a huge tree springs up, heavy with golden fruit. And soon all the land is fertile with fruits and grains. This area of Ireland is named for him: *Conneda*, or *Connacht.*

Grape

My only regret in life is that I didn't drink more wine.

—Ernest Hemingway

Botanical name: *Vitis* sp.

Native to: Caucasus, Iran, North America

Of note: The common species of grape used to make wine is *Vitus vinifera.* Several *Vitis* are native to North America. *V. californica* is a species of grape indigenous to California. Another species, *V. riparia,* is found in North America, across central and eastern Canada, and central and eastern United States.

Medicinal properties: Grapes are high in antioxidants and contain phytochemicals, including resveratrol, which has been shown to reduce the risk of heart disease and lower blood pressure. They are anti-inflammatory, anticarcinogenic, and antimicrobial.

Magical properties: Prosperity, fertility, abundance. Grapes represent the ripening of harvest and so represent dreams into fruition. A good harvest also represents abundance and prosperity, so grapes can attract and maintain both. Grapes and their products, including raisins and wine, can be used in ritual consumption and placed on altars as offerings.

The Lore

Where there are grapes, there is wine. The first known grape wine came from the Caucasus and Iran but made its way into Greece around 4500 BCE. Dionysus, the son of Zeus and a mortal woman named Semele, is associated with wine and therefore grapes, his own chariot bedecked with grapevines. Zeus killed Semele, but only by a trick of Hera, who had convinced Semele to ask Zeus to visit in his "full thunderous glory." When he did, Semele instantly burned up, but not before Zeus saved their child, whom he secreted away to be raised by nymphs in the Valley of Nysa, far away from Hera's wrath. Dionysus showed the farmers of the valley how to plant and tend grapes and how to turn the grapes into wine at harvest. But trouble came when Dionysus was kidnapped by pirates, who thought he was a wealthy prince for whom they could get a hefty ransom. The pirates tried to tie Dionysus to the mast, but the ropes instantly fell away, a fact one of the crew took note of and, in a panic, shouted that the boy must be a god to have such powers. The rest of the crew ignored the warning cry, until Dionysus blew his wine-o breath across the ship, filling the sails and the deck with blood red wine. The startled crew quickly threw themselves overboard. Upon hitting the water, the men transformed into dolphins and swam away. Dionysus, like alcohol itself, could incite his followers to riots and frenzy. It is said women were especially vulnerable to his wild ways, even abandoning their children and leaving their families to become disciples of Dionysus.

Dionysus's Roman counterpart, Bacchus, is the god of wine and agriculture and therefore fertility and merrymaking. In Greek and Roman mythology, Dionysus and Bacchus are nearly identical; both are in charge of revelry and responsible for the inevitable chaos that ensues. Another Roman god, Liber or Liber Pater, shares many of the same qualities as both Dionysus and Bacchus. The Roman festival of Bacchus, known as Bacchanalia, is held mid-March. An unbridled celebration, where wanton displays of lust and debauchery are elevated to a ritualistic status, it's hardly surprising that the powers-that-be tried to ban the festival and punish the followers of Bacchus. Little did they suspect that the very principle of Bacchanalia would live on today every Saturday night.

If we lose our moral compass in the presence of Bacchus/Dionysus, fear not, for we find it again in Aesop and the classic fable "The Fox and the Grapes."

One summer's morning a fox was strolling through an orchard when he came upon a particularly beautiful bunch of grapes, ripened to perfection in the summer sun. The vine had been trained to grow up and over the tree, and the bunch of grapes was dangling high above. "Just the thing to quench my thirst," thought the fox. He could see he would not be able to reach the grapes, so he got a running start and took a giant leap but missed the grapes. He drew back further, with an even greater running start, but again he was not able to reach the tempting grapes. The fox continued at this for several more attempts, so desperate for those juicy grapes was he. But eventually, he had to give up. And so, he walked away with his nose in the air, saying: "I am sure they are sour." It is easy to despise what you cannot get.

Indigenous peoples of California use the wild grape in a number of ways, both as a food source and for medicine. The roots can be steeped in water to make a decoction used as a blood purifier. The roots are also made into a tea as an emetic and a cathartic. The Hupa use the fiber of the roots for basket making; the Maidu (*To si dum*) use the stem to bind the edge of baskets. The Miwok traditionally line earth ovens with the leaves. The Southwestern Pomo use the vines as ties and "to make a hoop on a baby basket."

The late Patricia Monaghan, in her book *Encyclopedia of Goddesses and Heroines*, reminds readers of Ninkasi, a Sumerian goddess of intoxicating fruit—grapes in particular. One of her seven children grew up to be the goddess of beer.

Originating in Spain but now practiced in Spanish-speaking countries around the world, there is a long-standing tradition of eating twelve grapes as the clock strikes midnight on New Year's Eve. This custom will bring luck, with each grape representing a month of the year to come. Following this tradition will ward off bad luck and bring prosperity.

There is a funny little tale of Hungarian descent, the "Talking Grapes." In the story, a king has three daughters.

Before he headed to market, the king asked his daughters what they would like him to bring them back. The eldest asked for a gown of gold; the middle daughter, a gown of silver; but the youngest said she wanted "talking grapes, a smiling apple, and a tinkling apricot." At market the king found the gowns but could not find these fruits for his youngest. As he headed home, his carriage became stuck in the mud. Along came a pig who offered to help the king get unstuck if he promised the pig his youngest daughter. The king, who was in a bit of a panic and anxious to return home, agreed without thinking. The pig pushed the carriage out of the mud, and the king headed home with the gowns, but nothing for his youngest and a looming promise on the horizon. The next day the pig arrived at the king's palace and asked for the promised daughter. The king tried to trick the pig by sending down a peasant girl dressed in silks, but the pig was not fooled. So the king sent down the

youngest daughter dressed in rags, but the pig was not fooled and took her away in a wheelbarrow. The pig brought her to a pigsty, where the girl, exhausted from crying all day and the bumpy ride, fell asleep on a bed of straw. Imagine her astonishment when she woke the next day in a fairy-like palace, attended by maids. She dressed and headed into the garden, where she was met by a handsome young man who told her all she saw was hers. She turned and heard the grapes talk to her, "Pick us and eat us!" they cried. Then she saw an apple smiling at her and heard an apricot tinkling. The prince had been bewitched into a pig, and the only way to end the enchantment was to meet a woman who wished for talking grapes. They lived happily, abundantly, ever after.

To dream of grapes foretells to the maiden that her husband will be a cheerful companion and a great songster. They denote much happiness in marriage and success in trade. If you are in love, they augur a speedy union between you and your sweetheart.
— *The Witches' Book of Dreams*

Hyacinth

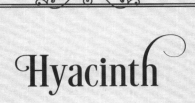

If I had but two loaves of bread, I would sell one and buy hyacinths, for they would feed my soul.

—Mohammad

Botanical name: *Hyacinthus orientalis*

Native to: The Mediterranean, central and southern Turkey, tropical Africa, Lebanon, northwestern Syria

Also called: Dutch hyacinth, common hyacinth, garden hyacinth

Medicinal properties: Anticancer. In traditional medicine the whole plant, including the leaves and the bulbs, is used to treat wounds and aid in healing prostate disease and hemorrhoids. The plant contains anthocyanins known for having antioxidant, anti-inflammatory, and antimutagenic effects. A 2021 study conducted by the National Institutes of Health explored the anticancer properties of hyacinths and found the results to reveal that hyacinths exhibit high potential to both stimulate the immune system and inhibit cancer growth.

Magical properties: Happiness, everlasting love, immortality. Hyacinth will bond two people in friendship or as lovers. Gift a hyacinth to someone to seal the the deal. Author Lilith Dorsey tells us a growing hyacinth bulb in the bedroom can prevent nightmares.

The Lore

I will never forget the spring when I was twenty-five and living in Amsterdam. Snow had fallen in early February, a thin sheet of ice forming on water in the canals. It seemed that one minute I was shivering on a bike, commuting to a black-market job I am sworn to secrecy over, and the next I was inhaling the rich floral scent of hyacinths. They really seemed to be everywhere, all at once. The Netherlands are known for their bulb exports (see the section on tulips), so it should have come as no surprise to me that in every median and public park scores upon scores of hyacinths were bursting into the early spring air. To this day, when I smell a hyacinth, I'm transported back to the cobblestone sidewalks of that beautiful city.

The name *Hyacinth* comes from a dramatic Greek myth involving two worlds of winter and summer: King Amyclas's youngest son, Hyacinthus; and Apollo, the god of music, poetry, and arts. Apollo fell in love with Hyacinthus and his natural beauty and wished to spend all the time he could with Hyacinthus. One day, the two of them were playing discus. Apollo threw the discus so far it went up into the clouds. Hyacinthus stepped up to make his own throw, eager to impress Apollo, and was struck down by Apollo's disc. As Hyacinthus lay dying in Apollo's arms, Apollo declared that Hyacinthus would live on in the form of a flower that would come back every year. It would bloom and be fragrant, but fleeting, dying just as quickly as Hyacinthus himself. The flower became known as the Hyacinth. Wild hyacinths are said to have markings that look like the Greek letters *AI*, the sound of a mournful cry.

The Spartans celebrated Hyacinthia, a festival held in July honoring the duality of nature. The first day was spent in grief for the dead and for the death of vegetation, with sacrifices being made at the gravesite of Hyacinthus. The second day was one of revelry, honoring Apollo with singing, dancing, and games and celebrating the joy of the harvest.

It is not surprising then, that magically, hyacinths are associated with enchantments of happiness, protection, and everlasting love. A word of caution to would-be harvesters of hyacinth: the bulbs of hyacinths contain a substance that can cause an allergic reaction in some handlers, usually itching and a rash. When I worked in a retail nursery, we always handled bulbs with gloves and encouraged our customers to do the same.

Of the beloved flowers of a queen's cultivated bed, the hyacinth is prized for its beauty and fragrance. First introduced from Turkey to much of Europe and England in 1573, it became popular enough that by 1725 there were already over two hundred cultivars. Though it never invoked the feverish desires of the tulip, it was—and is—widely cherished even today.

In "Little Ida's Flowers" a short story from Hans Christian Andersen, hyacinths, roses, and lilies take center stage, and they take on great personalities. Andersen's story was first published in 1835, and I cannot help but wonder if this story influenced Lewis Carroll's chapter "The Garden of Live Flowers" in his 1871 *Through the Looking Glass*, the sequel to the wildly popular *Alice's Adventures in Wonderland*. The 1951 Disney film *Alice in Wonderland* was based on both books, specifically borrowing the flower chapter for Alice's adventures.

> *"They are inside the palace now," replied the student. "As soon as the king and all his court go back to the town, the flowers hasten out of the garden and into the palace, where they have famous times. Oh, if you could but see them! The two most beautiful roses seat themselves on the throne and act king and queen. All the tall red cockscombs stand before them on either side and bow; they are the chamberlains. Then all the pretty flowers come, and there is a great ball. The blue violets represent the naval cadets; they dance with hyacinths and crocuses, who take the part of young ladies. The tulips and the tall tiger lilies are old ladies,—dowagers,—who see to it that the dancing is well done and that all things go on properly."*

Lily

The modest Rose puts forth a thorn,
The humble sheep a threat'ning horn:
While the Lily white shall in love delight,
Nor a thorn nor a threat stain her beauty bright.

—William Blake, "The Lily"

Botanical name: *Lilium* spp.

Native to: Asia, Americas, Middle East, Balkans

Medicinal properties: A sedative and tonic. For centuries the bulbs have been ground and mixed with honey as a topical treatment for infections, snake bites, bruises, blemishes, and wrinkles. Pliny the Elder mentions boiling the bulbs to make a treatment for corns and calluses.

Magical properties: Purity, immortality. The Easter lily and the Madonna lily represent resurrection and purity; however, lilies were once in the domain of Hera. Because of this, they can be used in both fertility and rebirth rituals. I use fresh, fragrant lilies on the altar when doing any self-resurrection or abundance work.

The Lore

It is almost unfair to dedicate a section titled simply "Lily" because the lily family itself is incredibly large. A native to the Middle East and Balkans, the Madonna lily (*Lilium candidum*), also called the meadow lily or white lily, has been used in folk medicine for centuries and is now being studied for its antidiabetic and anti-inflammatory properties. The Asiatic lilies (*L. aratum* or *L. Asiatic*) come in a stunning array of colors from pure white to deep maroon and every shade in between. Similar, though smaller, species of lilies are native to the Americas, including my favorite the rare Humboldt lily (*L. humboldtii*). The root of this plant is edible. In *Plants Used by the Indians of Mendocino County, California,* V. K. Chestnut writes, "Nowhere in the world is there a more characteristic abundance and variety of bulbous-rooted liliaceous plants than in California." And of those many plants, nearly all have edible roots.

In Greek mythology, lilies fell under the domain of Hera. After being tricked into suckling an infant Heracles, she tore him from her breast, scattering the milk. Some of this flew to the skies and formed the Milky Way. Some milk scattered onto Earth and from the droplets sprouted lilies.

Tiger lilies are a fascinating flower, glorious and bold in the garden. Most often, the tiger lily sold in catalogs and stores is the Asiatic variety (*L. lancifolium*). They are brilliant orange with little spots, recalling the colors of the Asian tiger. However, there are many species of tiger lilies in the Americas, from the prairies of Minnesota to the foothills of California. Sometimes called leopard lilies, they range from deep orange to pale yellow, all with the signature spots and prominent stamen.

In the second chapter of Lewis Carroll's Alice sequel, *Through the Looking Glass and What Alice Found There*, Carroll brings to life a buzzy flower garden. He personifies the flowers in a manner that suggests he'd spent some time contemplating the individual floral personalities. The ferocious tiger lily, the vain rose, the obnoxious daisies. Alice wandered into this garden, thinking it was like a garden back home. Little did she know, it was enchanted.

"O Tiger-lily," said Alice, addressing herself to one that was waving gracefully about in the wind, "I wish you could talk!"

"We can talk," said the Tiger-lily: "when there's anybody worth talking to."

Alice was so astonished that she could not speak for a minute: it quite seemed to take her breath away. At length, as the Tiger-lily only went on waving about, she spoke again, in a timid voice—almost in a whisper. "And can all the flowers talk?"

"As well as you can," said the Tiger-lily. "And a great deal louder."

"It isn't manners for us to begin, you know," said the Rose, "and I really was wondering when you'd speak! Said I to myself, 'Her face has got some sense in it, though it's not a clever one!' Still, you're the right colour, and that goes a long way."

"I don't care about the colour," the Tiger-lily remarked. "If only her petals curled up a little more, she'd be all right."

Alice didn't like being criticised, so she began asking questions. "Aren't you sometimes frightened at being planted out here, with nobody to take care of you?"

"There's the tree in the middle," said the Rose: "what else is it good for?"

"But what could it do, if any danger came?" Alice asked.

"It says 'Bough-wough!'" cried a Daisy: "that's why its branches are called boughs!"

"Didn't you know that?" cried another Daisy, and here they all began shouting together, till the air seemed quite full of little shrill voices. "Silence, every one of you!" cried the Tiger-lily, waving itself passionately from side to side, and trembling with excitement. "They know I can't get at them!" it panted, bending its quivering head towards Alice, "or they wouldn't dare to do it!"

"Never mind!" Alice said in a soothing tone, and stooping down to the daisies, who were just beginning again, she whispered, "If you don't hold your tongues, I'll pick you!"

There was silence in a moment, and several of the pink daisies turned white.

"That's right!" said the Tiger-lily. "The daisies are worst of all. When one speaks, they all begin together, and it's enough to make one wither to hear the way they go on!"

"How is it you can all talk so nicely?" Alice said, hoping to get it into a better temper by a compliment. "I've been in many gardens before, but none of the flowers could talk."

"Put your hand down, and feel the ground," said the Tiger-lily. "Then you'll know why."

Alice did so. "It's very hard," she said, "but I don't see what that has to do with it."

"In most gardens," the Tiger-lily said, "they make the beds too soft—so that the flowers are always asleep."

This sounded a very good reason, and Alice was quite pleased to know it. "I never thought of that before!" she said.

"It's my opinion that you never think at all," the Rose said in a rather severe tone.

"I never saw anybody that looked stupider," a Violet said, so suddenly, that Alice quite jumped; for it hadn't spoken before.

"Hold your tongue!" cried the Tiger-lily. "As if you ever saw anybody! You keep your head under the leaves, and snore away there, till you know no more what's going on in the world, than if you were a bud!"

"Are there any more people in the garden besides me?" Alice said, not choosing to notice the Rose's last remark.

"There's one other flower in the garden that can move about like you," said the Rose. "I wonder how you do it—" ("You're always wondering," said the Tiger-lily), "but she's more bushy than you are."

"Is she like me?" Alice asked eagerly, for the thought crossed her mind, "There's another little girl in the garden, somewhere!"

"Well, she has the same awkward shape as you," the Rose said, "but she's redder— and her petals are shorter, I think."

"Her petals are done up close, almost like a dahlia," the Tiger-lily interrupted: "not tumbled about anyhow, like yours."

"But that's not your fault," the Rose added kindly: "you're beginning to fade, you know—and then one can't help one's petals getting a little untidy."

Alice didn't like this idea at all: so, to change the subject, she asked "Does she ever come out here?"

"I daresay you'll see her soon," said the Rose. "She's one of the thorny kind."

The color of the lily can have great significance toward the meaning of the flower. A white lily represents purity, making it a standard flower for weddings and for funerals. Yellow lilies represent a lie or falsehood, or simply, joy.

Narcissus

Come and let us seek together.
Springtime lore of daffodils,
Giving to the golden weather
Greeting on the sun-warm hills.

—Lucy Maud Montgomery, "Spring Song"

Botanical name: *Narcissus* sp.

Native to: Southern Europe and northern Africa

Also called: Daffodils, narcissus, paper whites, jonquil

Medicinal properties: Narcissus are known to shorten the life of other cut flowers, likely due to the presence of calcium oxalate in the sap, which has been used in folk medicine to heal wounds although it is also an irritant. The bulbs have a growth inhibitor, and for this reason, the use of narcissus in the management of cancer is under study. Both the flowers and bulbs are anticarcinogens and antibiotics. It's worth noting the flowers are considered poisonous, so caution should be used in any internal medicinal use.

Magical properties: Narcissus and daffodils make a powerful ingredient in spells for love and beauty. Additionally, use them in rituals for self-love and healing. As spring flowers, they are naturally associated with renewal and fertility. Narcissus also tend to naturalize, meaning they come back year after year and spread on their own. This gives them a quality of resilience, so employ them magically to overcoming obstacles and find your place in the world. The heavy scent of narcissus may have a sedative quality, helping with the transition to the Underworld. Use narcissus to connect with those who have passed away.

Of note: There are more than fifty species of flowering bulbs that fall within the genus *Narcissus* and an endless number of hybrids. This large number results in a vast array of color combinations and flower sizes. Daffodils are the most common—their signature large, bright yellow blooms a signal to the world that spring has arrived. *Narcissus jonquilla,* or simply jonquil or jonquil daffodils, are a close second. They tend to have smaller double flowers that grow more numerous. And paperwhites, which are frequently just referred to as narcissus, are the most fragrant of the bulbs, often "forced" in pebbles indoors around the holidays as a gift. Their name comes from their color and the paper-thin petals. In summary, daffodils are jonquils are also narcissus. But narcissus are not necessarily daffodils or jonquils.

The Lore

In the foothills of California, traces of the Gold Rush are everywhere. Of a time when people came in droves to blast away the hills and rake the rivers looking for the elusive shiny nugget. With population boom, so comes disease and death, and for every once-booming mining town, a remote pioneer cemetery hides among the pines. Many of these graves have a common flower every spring: the bright yellow daffodil.

When I was little, I would sit beside a crop of daffodils in the cemetery and pretend the daffodils' trumpet-like corona was the perfect transmitter. I would never pick the flowers, believing instead that I could speak to the fairies through this magical telephone. Or perhaps directly underground to the dead themselves. In much of Celtic fairy mythology, the Otherworld and the Underworld are one and the same. Maybe my young brain was on to something.

> *I wandered lonely as a cloud.*
> *That floats on high o'er vales and hills,*
> *When all at once I saw a crowd,*
> *A host of golden Daffodils*
> —William Wadsworth, "Daffodils"

The name *Narcissus* comes from the Greek story of Narcissus and Echo. Narcissus, the son of the river god Cephissus and the water nymph Liriope, was so handsome that even as a young child he was cautioned to never look upon himself. Mirrors and gazing pools were kept from him, for the fear was that were he to see someone so handsome, he could never love another as much as he loved himself. Like many before her, Echo was in love with Narcissus. But Narcissus was not interested in her and rejected her. In her sorrow, Echo faded away, leaving behind nothing more than the whisper of her voice, what we today call the *echo*. Echo's dying whisper was heard by the goddess Nemesis, who, fittingly, extracted revenge on Echo's behalf. Nemesis made it so that Narcissus would happen upon a spring in which he would see his reflection. Instantly, he fell in love with the handsome devil staring back at him. Narcissus stared into his own eyes, admired his own chiseled features and fine head of hair, until so much time passed that he took no food nor drink. He too wasted away, dying looking at his own reflection. His body sank into the ground, and the following year in the spot where he died, the Narcissus flower bloomed. To this day we use the term *narcissist* to mean someone who is self-absorbed and self-obsessed. In some versions of the story, the flowers spring out directly from his corpse. The cup in the center of the flower is said to hold the tears of Narcissus.

In Lang's *The Green Fairy Book*, we find an entirely different story about a prince named Narcissus. In it, we find several important features of a good fairy tale: love—unrequited or blossoming; the means to make oneself invisible through either a piece of clothing or jewelry; a supernatural power that allows the hero to bestow gifts, transform, or stop time; and a challenge or evil challenger to the happiness of whatever love is trying to bloom.

In this case Prince Narcissus was orphaned when his parents, the king and queen, died and he was left under the care of a fairy named Melinette.

> *In this they did very well for him, for the Fairy was as kind as she was powerful, and she spared no pains in teaching the little Prince everything it was good for him to know, and even imparted to him some of her own Fairy lore. But as soon as he was grown up she sent him out to see the world for himself, though all the time she was secretly keeping watch over him, ready to help in any time of need. Before he started she gave him a ring which would render him invisible when he put it on his finger. These rings seem to be quite common; you must often have heard of them, even if you have never seen one.*

He fell in love with a princess named Potentilla, "as she sat by the brook, weaving a garland of blue forget-me-nots to crown her waving golden locks." What could possibly go wrong, then? He courted her as just a voice, eventually removing the ring and enchanting her with his handsomeness. One day an Enchanter came along, a wizard who was a little worse for wear in his second-best cloak and a hulking frame. He startled the poor princess, who was waiting for her handsome prince to reappear. She cried, "Oh! Where is my Narcissus?"

> *To which he replied with a self-satisfied chuckle, "You want a narcissus, madam? Well, they are not rare; you shall have as many as you like!"*

> *Whereupon he waved his wand, and the Princess found herself surrounded and half buried in the fragrant flowers.*

The Enchanter sought to possess Princess Potentilla, but the fairy Melinette came to her defense. But the Enchanter and Narcissus began to vie for Potentilla's heart in a series of outrageous feats, such as commanding all the birds in the domain, or making the river boil up with mud. When the Enchanter failed to convince her, he put a spell on her and put her to sleep. While she slept, he headed to her parents and convinced them he should marry her. With the help of the fairies, Narcissus arrived in the nick of time and rescued Princess Potentilla from her hazy state, and they escaped into the afternoon sun.

Many witches believe daffodils to be a powerful ingredient in love spells and beauty, but exercise caution should you "go too far." Additionally, narcissus species are toxic and should never be consumed in cooking or teas. Folkard writes, "Fates wore wreaths of the Narcissus, and the Greeks twined the white stars of the odorous blossoms among the tangled locks of the Eumenides." The Eumenides, also known as the Furies, were Greek deities of revenge. A crown of narcissus flowers was woven in honor of these vengeful gods, and these crowns were placed upon the heads of the dead. There are several accounts of a recipe from the island of Guernsey that will allow you to see a sorcerer for who they are. Put the roots of both small and large sage, the pith of elder, and daffodil bulbs together in vinegar and ensure that the concoction comes to a boil at exactly a quarter of an hour before noon. As the bubbles appear, the sorcerer will make an appearance, but you must leave the door open.

Daffy down dilly
Has come to town
In a yellow petticoat
And a green gown
—Children's nursery rhyme

Pomegranate

Once when I was living in the heart of a pomegranate, I heard a seed
saying, "Someday I shall become a tree, and the wind will sing in
my branches, and the sun will dance on my leaves, and I shall be
strong and beautiful through all the seasons."

—Kahlil Gibran, "The Pomegranate"

Botanical name: *Punica granatum*

Native to: Iran, northern India

Also called: Pomegranate; *grenade* (French); *rodie* (Romanian); *granaatappel* (Dutch); *melograno* (Italian)

Of note: Several miniature varieties such as *P. granatum 'Nana'* are grown as ornamentals and do not produce particularity viable fruit; however, they can make beautiful additions to a magical garden or botanical altar.

Medicinal properties: Medicinally, the pomegranate is a vermifugal, meaning it can be used to rid the body of parasites. Specifically, a strong tea of the bark can treat tapeworms. The rind is high in tannins and therefore astringent. Diluted, it can be a wash for skin infections, a gargle for throat irritation, and can treat diarrhea and vaginal infections. Be sure to use the right amount, though, because in strong doses it can induce vomiting. The seeds and juice of the pomegranate have antioxidants, a nod to its immortal role in lore. The edible parts also contain vitamin C, potassium, and magnesium. The juice lowers blood pressure and cholesterol and is even being studied for its anticancer potential.

Magical properties: Pomegranates represent abundance, fertility, prosperity, hope, and unity. Pomegranates also represent resurrection and immortality and can be used in working with the dead. The association with blood makes pomegranate juice an excellent substitute for blood in rituals. It can also be used for menstrual or cyclical magical work. In Italy, divining rods were made of pomegranate, used to help find buried treasure. Because it is resistant to worms, the pomegranate also represents resilience.

The Lore

The pomegranate, with its crimson jewel-like seeds, is a fruit that leaves you wrought with desire. An abundant, vivid interior is packed with luscious but elusive seeds. Eating a pomegranate is time consuming when you pull out seeds and eat them one by one. You cannot simply rip into a pomegranate as you would an apple or suck the juices dry as with an orange. There is a sacred almost-dissatisfying patience that comes with the pomegranate.

It is a common belief around the world that whether entering the fairy kingdom or the Underworld, you should not under any circumstance eat or drink *anything*. If you do, you may become enchanted and bound to that world, perhaps by mysterious plant toxins in the food or drink, or perhaps simply by taking something from the Otherworld, entering you into an immediate debt. In no story is that more clearly demonstrated than the story of Persephone, the daughter of Zeus and Demeter—the goddess of agriculture and plants.

Persephone was kidnapped by Hades and dragged down to the Underworld. Horrified, she tried to leave to return to her mother and the earthly realm, but she was either tricked or tempted by the pomegranate. Some say Hades fed her the seeds of the pomegranate; others that he simply put the irresistible fruit in her path. Either way, the weary Persephone made a tiny meal of six little seeds. Each of these seeds sealed her fate, binding her to the Underworld for six months of the year.

When her mother found out, including that dear old Zeus conspired with Hades to kidnap Persephone, she was livid and caused all the plants on Earth to wither and die. This represents winter, when Persephone must bide her time in the darkness, waiting for the return of spring when she is reunited with her mother. Variations on this myth frame Persephone as the one to blame for her own fate, saying that her inability to resist the pomegranate was her own undoing, not dissimilar to the way Eve is blamed for eating the fruit of temptation. Many scholars suggest it was the pomegranate, not the apple, that was the forbidden fruit in the Garden of Eden, tying these two stories together in the annals of mythology.

And her sweet red lips on these lips of mine
Burned like the ruby fire set
In the swinging lamp of a crimson shrine,
Or the bleeding wounds of the pomegranate,
Or the heart of the lotus drenched and wet
With the spilt-out blood of the rose-red wine.
— Oscar Wilde, "In the Gold Room"

Pomegranates are also sacred to Ishtar (earlier known as Inanna), the Sumerian goddess of healing and medicine, and Gula, the Sumerian goddess of death. Their priestesses were unmarried women dedicated to helping the sick and dying. Among their practices, they would bury pomegranates beneath the floors of the homes of sick people to ward off disease. Pomegranates here represent resurrection and immortality, an aid for the ill in this life and the dead in the afterlife.

Although we associate the pomegranate with Persephone, the tree originates in Bacchus's domain. Bacchus (Dionysus), whom we met earlier in the section on grapes, was an agricultural god known for his affiliation with wine, celebration, and harvest. The story goes that there was a lovely nymph who was told by a prophet that she was destined to wear a crown. Rather than be tied down and marry this nymph to crown her as queen, he instead transformed her into a beautiful tree, the pomegranate tree, whose fruits each sport a crown. Win-win, right?

Another Greek myth describes a young woman whose widowed father gave her unwanted attention. She dies by suicide, no doubt to escape his predatory nature. The Gods took pity on her and transformed her dying body into the pomegranate tree.

And then there is the story of Agdistis, an ancient intersex deity born with both male and female reproductive organs. In some versions the wound was self-inflicted; in others the deity was tricked by a jealous Dionysus; but both versions are gruesome as the male genitalia were either torn or cut off. The blood that flowed from this wound fertilized the ground and out of this came the pomegranate tree, the blood-red juice of the fruit representing Agdistis's blood. Menoeceus was a The-ban named for his grandfather who died by suicide as commanded by the oracle at Delphi. From his tomb grows a pomegranate tree, and the juice inside the fruit is akin to his blood.

The association with the pomegranate and blood goes back to the Egyp-tians, where it is said that Ra was able to satisfy the bloodlust of Sekhmet with pomegranate juice. Sekhmet, the Egyptian goddess of war, chaos, and destruc-tion—but also healing—was tricked into ending a battle. Ra filled thousands of jugs with pomegranate wine, and Sekhmet, believing it was the blood from the battle, guzzled it down. Satiated, and a little drunk, she ended her torrent of destruction. This story recalls the Hindu goddess Kali, whose teeth were red with blood after battling demons, as red as pomegranate flowers. A symbol of both resurrection and immortality, the pomegranate is also considered one of abundance and fertility. Ganesh, the elephant-headed Hindu god, is frequently depicted with a pomegranate in his hand. In fact, the association with Ganesh is so strong that there is a commercial cultivar of pomegranate known as *Punica granatum 'Ganesh,'* which is known for producing a heavy crop of large fruits with a pinkish rind.

It seems that almost universally, pomegranate is revered as a symbol for resurrection, immortality, and fertility. When used on gravestones and depicted as a whole fruit, it is associated with everlasting life. If the seeds are shown, they represent hope, unity, love, passion, and abundance. This can also be true when used symbolically in artwork.

Medicinally, pomegranate juice may help prevent high blood pressure and treat heart disease, high cholesterol, and diabetes. Some studies have found anticancer properties in the pomegranate. According to Joseph E. Meyer in his seminal work *The Herbalist*, the flowers, rind, and root bark all have medicinal properties. The flowers and bark are astringent and were once used to treat tapeworm as well as throat irritation. Interesting tidbit: Meyer founded the Indiana Botanic Garden, the largest and oldest purveyor of herbal goods in the United States. Started in 1910, it still operates today. He also published *The Herbalist Almanac* beginning in 1925.

In the *Tales of the Arabian Nights*, Scheherazade tells stories to ward off the advances of her husband, who by then had a reputation for marrying virgins, bedding them on the wedding night, and killing them the next morning so they couldn't betray him. To keep him from wishing her dead, she tells stories night after night, each one ending in suspense so that he cannot kill her because he wants to know the ending. Most famous of these is the story of Aladdin, followed by Sinbad the Sailor. But also among these stories are those of the three Calenders—friar-like wanderers who travel the lands sharing wisdom and stories. In this story, the Calenders are actually disposed kings who are seeking help to restore their kingdoms. They are dressed alike in simple robes with long, twisted mustaches, clean-shaven chins, and each having lost one eye. They are implored to tell the story of how they came to be poor, one-eyed wanderers. Each in turn tells their story of how they came to lose their kingdom, but it is the second Calender whose story is most intriguing. It features shapeshifting and an Underworld-like place.

In his story, the second Calender was out with his men when they were set upon by robbers. Separated, the king was taken in by a tailor who lived in the forest. One day, while exploring the woods around the tailor's home, he discovered a trap door at the base of a tree. He pulled on a brass ring, which opened the door and revealed a staircase. It led to an underground palace where a beautiful woman resided. She had a jealous husband who kept her shut away there and visited every ten days unless she called upon him by pressing a panel in the wall. She implored the young king to stay with her for the remaining days until her husband returned. He, of course, fell in love with her beauty and, drunk on wine, decided he must take her away from her prison-palace. In his passion, he accidentally kicked the panel that summoned the husband. The jealous husband killed his wife, caught in the act, by beheading her and then transformed the young king into an ape. For a time, the man-ape dwelled in the woods alone, but eventually he stowed away on a passing ship. The ship's crew were taken aback by the ape's intelligence. The ape quickly made a name for himself as a scribe. All who met him were astounded that he could read and write, so the crew hastened to provide him with pen, ink, and parchment. Then they brought him to the king, who in turn invited the ape-man to stay at the palace. During a game of chess, the king's daughter appeared. Within minutes, she summoned a demon spirit called an *afrit* (also spelled *efrite, efreet, ifrit,* and sometimes *afree*) from the land of the dead. The spirit was annoyed at being called forth. Cue the magical battle.

"You've betrayed me! You promised never to summon me again," insisted the afrit.

"I promised no such thing!" she declared.

The afrit then transformed itself into a lion and leapt at her. She pulled a lock of her own hair and blew on it, creating a sharp-bladed sword, which she used to cut off the lion's head. From where the head was immediately sprung forth a scorpion. So, the woman became a snake, chasing after the scorpion, which then shapeshifted

into an eagle. But the lady outsmarted him and became a vulture, and the two continued fighting. The eagle became a cat and the lady-vulture a wolf. The fight continued, with the black panther and the wolf nearly equal until the cat, exhausted,
shapeshifted into a pomegranate and rolled away. The wolf pounced on it, upon
which the pomegranate rose up and burst, scattering little blood-red seeds all over
the floor. The wolf transformed into a rooster and began pecking at all the little
seeds, but there was one he could not find. At last, he spied the seed on the edge of a
little indoor pool. Just as he came to reach it, the seed fell into the water and became
a fish. The rooster became another fish and dove in after it, with the water churning
and foaming in their frenzy. Out of this roiling water came the afrit, with eyes aflame,
pursued quickly by the daughter, who was also emitting fire from her eyes and nose
and mouth. They shot arrows of fire at one another until the room became so filled
with smoke that no one could see. The afrit blew flames at the king and the ape-man,
who lost his eye in the process. Not long after, the daughter emerged victorious,
with the afrit merely a heap of ashes at her feet.

The early French word for pomegranate was *grenade.*
This form is reflected in the botanical name today: *Punica
granatum.* It is also where we get *grenadine,* which is essentially
pomegranate syrup. It turns out that grenades were named
for pomegranates, as they were thought to look like the fruit.

Rose

Gather the rose of love whilst yet is time.

—Edmund Spenser, *The Faerie Queene*

Botanical name: *Rosa* sp.

Native to: Asia, also North America, Europe, Africa

Medicinal properties: Rose hips are high in vitamin C and antioxidants. Rose oil is used as a treatment for depression and anxiety. The most fragrant species, *R. damascena*, has been shown to have pharmacological properties as antidiabetic, antioxidant, antibacterial, and anti-HIV, among other healing effects. Culpeper describes numerous uses, including a treatment for insomnia, stomach troubles, and even congestion.

Magical properties: Roses are a universal symbol of love and loyalty and purity. Rose petals are still used traditionally to bless a marriage, often strewn along the path where the bride will walk; however, some folk traditions caution that red rose petals tossed in this manner are ill luck. Roses, rose petals, rose water, and rose oil can all be used in love spells. In German folklore, rose leaves can be thrown upon a coal fire for luck. Roses also represent beauty and are used in all manner of charms. A drop of your own blood left at the roots of a rose tree will help ensure rosy cheeks and a fine complexion. Roses, both cultivated and the wild briar rose, appear again and again in story and song as emblems of immortality. They are sometimes associated with early death, as in the song "Barbara Allen." Roses may also be used in death magic and passing-over rituals to represent both the fleeting beauty and impermanence of life, as the beautiful rose fades, and the scent of the rose invoking the loved ones from the beyond.

The Lore

On a recent trip to the Culloden battlefield near Inverness, Scotland, as we walked the well-worn paths through the field, our guide—a vibrant, animated woman—told us the story of how, after the battle, the ruling king's army made it a mission to destroy anyone who had been part of the Jacobite Uprising. As the militia headed from parcel to parcel, and cottage to cottage, they would knock upon the door and ask a simple, but loaded, question: "Do you garden?"

The answer to this would inevitably be yes, for everyone kept at least a cottage garden to feed their families, so the question was a trick. It also had layered meaning, for the symbol of Bonnie Prince Charles and the Jacobites was a white rose. Jacobites would plant the white rose in their front yards so that secret rebels who passed by would know they could find respite there. Were the militia looking not just for gardens but for white roses? The battle at Culloden took place on April 16, 1746. In the Highlands, though many a plant would be greening, it's possible—if not likely—that roses would not yet be in bloom, so the gardening question would be reason enough. A yes answer would leave the resident and their entire family killed. Still, by early June, the white roses would be flourishing. And the Jacobites were still being hunted.

Today, you will find white roses, *Rosa × alba*, growing throughout Scotland.

As I stood outside the croft on the Culloden fields, a phrase began to echo in my head. Could it be this which Lewis Carroll was alluding to when the pack of cards—the Five, the Seven, and the Two—were "painting the roses red"? Carroll was born in 1832, and *Alice's Adventures in Wonderland* was published in 1865. The land upon which the battle at Culloden took place was purchased by a private investor and the tower monument and clan stones placed at this time. The story of Culloden was known, then, along with the history of the Jacobites, though like much of history, what version you learn so often depends on who tells it.

Many readers over the years have put forth the theory that the Queen of Hearts is a parody of Queen Victoria, or perhaps more so an amalgamated parody of the royal family in general, incorporating the habitual beheadings of Henry VIII into the declaration of "Off with their heads!" Carroll writes:

> *A large rose-tree stood near the entrance of the garden: the roses growing on it were white, but there were three gardeners at it, busily painting them red. Alice thought this a very curious thing, and she went nearer to watch them, and just as she came up to them she heard one of them say, "Look out now, Five! Don't go splashing paint over me like that!"*
>
> *"I couldn't help it," said Five, in a sulky tone; "Seven jogged my elbow."*
>
> *On which Seven looked up and said, "That's right, Five! Always lay the blame on others!"*
>
> *"You'd better not talk!" said Five. "I heard the Queen say only yesterday you deserved to be beheaded!"*
>
> *"What for?" said the one who had spoken first.*
>
> *"That's none of your business, Two!" said Seven.*
>
> *"Yes, it is his business!" said Five, "and I'll tell him—it was for bringing the cook tulip-roots instead of onions."*
>
> *Seven flung down his brush, and had just begun "Well, of all the unjust things—" when his eye chanced to fall upon Alice, as she stood watching them, and he checked himself suddenly: the others looked round also, and all of them bowed low.*
>
> *"Would you tell me," said Alice, a little timidly, "why you are painting those roses?"*
>
> *Five and Seven said nothing, but looked at Two. Two began in a low voice, "Why the fact is, you see, Miss, this here ought to have been a red rose-tree, and we put a white one in by mistake; and if the Queen was to find it out, we should all have our heads cut off,*

you know. So, you see, Miss, we're doing our best, afore she comes to—" At this moment
Five, who had been anxiously looking across the garden, called out "The Queen! The
Queen!" and the three gardeners instantly threw themselves flat upon their faces. There
was a sound of many footsteps, and Alice looked round, eager to see the Queen.

Could Carroll have been referring to the necessity to "paint the white roses"—
aka staunch the rebellion—in order to satiate the Queen? It stands to reason that
even centuries later the Jacobites remain a thorn in the Crown's side.

The story we now associate with Snow White is based on a story the Grimm
Brothers called "Snowdrop," but in the story "Snow White and Rose Red" we find
roses used as comparison to unrivaled beauty:

There was once a poor widow who lived in a lonely cottage. In front of the cottage was
a garden wherein stood two rose-trees, one of which bore white and the other red roses.
She had two children who were like the two rose-trees, and one was called Snow-
white, and the other Rose-red. They were as good and happy, as busy and cheerful
as ever two children in the world were, only Snow-white was more quiet and gentle
than Rose-red. Rose-red liked better to run about in the meadows and fields seeking
flowers and catching butterflies; but Snow-white sat at home with her mother, and
helped her with her housework, or read to her when there was nothing to do.

The family befriended a bear who stretched out on their hearth through the
winter. In the summer he headed to the woods to protect his hidden treasures from
thieving dwarves. The two daughters happened upon a bear while gathering fire-
wood and soon discovered the bear to be the one they had cared for all winter long.
Of course, this bear turned out to be a King's son.

Snow-white was married to him, and Rose-red to his brother, and they divided
between them the great treasure which the dwarf had gathered together in his cave.
The old mother lived peacefully and happily with her children for many years. She
took the two rose-trees with her, and they stood before her window, and every year
bore the most beautiful roses, white and red.

In Hans Christian Andersen's 1839 story "The Elf of the Rose," he describes a creature who lived in a giant rose tree, but don't be fooled by this charming excerpt; there's all kinds of stabbing and burying beneath the rose tree in this one.

> *In the midst of a garden grew a rose-tree, in full blossom, and in the prettiest of all the roses lived an elf. He was such a little wee thing, that no human eye could see him. Behind each leaf of the rose he had a sleeping chamber. He was as well formed and as beautiful as a little child could be, and had wings that reached from his shoulders to his feet. Oh, what sweet fragrance there was in his chambers! and how clean and beautiful were the walls! for they were the blushing leaves of the rose.*

In Andersen's "The Greenies," we find rose-dwelling creatures of a different ilk. This one is told from the point of view of the rose's greatest enemy: aphids. Ants have a symbiotic relationship with aphids, aka plant lice, farming them, and Andersen describes that relationship in this little story. He writes:

> *"I was born on a rose leaf. I and all the regiment live on the rose tree. We live off it, in fact. But then it lives again in us, who belong to the higher order of created beings.*

> *"The human beings do not like us. They pursue and murder us with soapsuds. Oh, it is a horrid drink! I seem to smell it even now. You cannot think how dreadful it is to be washed when one was not made to be washed. Men! you who look at us with your severe, soapsud eyes, think a moment what our place in nature is: we are born upon the roses, we die in roses—our whole life is a rose poem. Do not, I beg you, give us a name which you yourselves think so despicable—the name I cannot bear to pronounce. If you wish to speak of us, call us 'the ants' milch cows—the rose-tree regiment—the little green things."*

In a decidedly darker turn, "The Rose Tree" is a story I first read in collection ironically named *Myths That Every Child Should Know*, compiled by Hamilton Wright Mabie, an American essayist and editor, in 1906. It has many similar plot points to the gruesome Grimm Brothers' story of the Juniper Tree (which you'll find in Chapter 5 on woodlands), but to summarize, a child is killed and buried beneath a rose tree, but the sibling and a little bird have their ultimate revenge.

Tulip

The tulips are too excitable, it is winter here.

—Sylvia Plath, "Tulips"

Botanical name: *Tulipa* spp.

Native to: Central Asia, Iran

Also called: Turk's cap; *tulipani* (Italian); *lalea* (Romanian); *tulp* (Dutch)

Medicinal properties: The flowers have been used as a poultice for bites, stings, itching, and general irritation. Internally, they have been used as a diuretic and an antiseptic, good for coughs and colds. Red and purple tulip petals were once used as blush or lip tint.

Magical properties: Tulips are considered beloved flowers to fairies and elves, who protect the flowers and those who grow them. These flowers are associated with love and renewal.

The Lore

It may seem hard to believe that such a humble flower as the tulip could create a frenzy known as Tulip Mania. As Mike Nash describes in his book *Tulipomania*, tulip bulbs were introduced to Europe in 1562, when a Flemish merchant found them among his shipment of cloth, mistook them for onions, ate half of them, and planted the rest in his garden bed. By the spring of 1563, those bulbs were blooming, and the neighborhood noticed. By 1634, it was full-on fever in regard to the tulip trade. People were spending 100,000 florins to get forty bulbs. As recorded by Charles MacKay in his book *Extraordinary Popular Delusions and the Madness of Crowds* in 1635, a single bulb of *Admiral Liefken* sold for 4,400 florins; *Admiral Van der Eyck* sold for 1,260 florins; *Viceroy* for 3,000 florins; and the highly sought after *Semper Augustus* was 5,500 florins. Keep in mind that at the time, one thousand pounds of cheese went for 120 florins. An entire suit of clothing could be purchased for 80 florins.

Before any of this happened, tulips were prized flowers among the Ottoman Empire. And there is a folk tale to go along with it. The story is that throughout the land of the Ottomans dragons once dwelled, and they bore witness to many battles where young soldiers were killed. The Turkish dragons were of a gentle nature and after each battle would weep over the corpses of those who had died. It is said that the very first tulip sprouted from a spot where the dragon's tears fell. The name *Tulip* comes from *Tulipan*, a word for turban, owing to the turban-like formation of the tulip's flower.

In the story of Thumbelina, a woman so desired a child that she went to a witch who told her to plant a little seed of barley corn in a flowerpot. The woman tended the little pot and then "out of the pot grew a little plant that looked like a tulip."

"What a beautiful flower!" exclaimed the woman, and she kissed the red and yellow petals; but as she kissed them the flower burst open. It was a real tulip, such as one can see any day; but in the middle of the blossom, on the green velvety petals, sat a little girl, quite tiny, trim, and pretty. She was scarcely half a thumb in height; so, they called her Thumbelina. An elegant, polished walnut-shell served Thumbelina as a cradle, the blue petals of a violet were her mattress, and a roseleaf her coverlid. There she lay at night, but in the day-time she used to play about on the table; here the woman had put a bowl, surrounded by a ring of flowers, with their stalks in water, in the middle of which floated a great tulip petal, and on this Thumbelina sat, and sailed from one side of the bowl to the other, rowing herself with two white horse-hairs for oars. It was such a pretty sight! She could sing, too, with a voice more soft and sweet than had ever been heard before.

Today there are nearly three thousand different types of tulips, and they come in nearly every color of the rainbow. While botanists have tried to create a blue tulip, they've only succeeded in shades of purple.

CHAPTER 2

The Cottage Garden of Earthly Delights

Humble Foods in Story and Legend

BEAN • CABBAGE • CORN • GARLIC • PUMPKIN • TURNIP

Lettuce Turnip on Thyme

Let us walk beyond the courtyard of knotwork hedges and carefully tended roses and head round back to the kitchen garden. This humble little growing ground is buzzing with activity; there's always something to do in a vegetable garden. Pull a few weeds while you sample the fresh heads of lettuce. Mind your step on the path as the pumpkins have begun to take over. This is the kitchen garden, and it extends beyond little earthen beds and pots of rosemary into the corn fields and turnip rows beyond.

And though this garden may look more ordinary, it has secrets of its own. What may at first seem to be everyday foods have more than just vitamins and carbohydrates. Here you'll find legends of vampires and bewitched cabbage heads. If you're quiet, you might hear Stingy Jack shamble by. You'll climb beanstalks, and cabbage stalks, up into the sky. Take up your basket and start harvesting. There are magical tales waiting in every garden bed.

Bean

Beans, beans, the magical fruit
The more you eat, the more you toot,
The more you toot, the better you feel,
So eat beans at every meal!

—Every school child in America

Botanical name: *Phaseolus* spp.

Native to: North, Central, and South America; East Asia

Also called: frijoles (Spanish); mashkodesimin or miskodiisimin (Anishinaabe); tu-ya (Ani-Yunʼwiyaʼ/Cherokee)

Of note: The common bean (*Phaseolus vulgaris*) is grown around the world. Many species of beans are native to the United States, Mexico, and Central America, including the tepary bean (*P. acutifolius*) and the scarlet runner bean (*P. coccineus*). I call out these two species because they are included in the stories presented here. There is another bean crop, also called the broad bean or fava bean (*Vicia faba*), which is the primary bean known in Europe prior to colonization of the Americas.

Medicinal properties: Primarily used as a food crop, beans are rich in amino acids, protein, and other nutrients and have been shown to lower cholesterol and blood pressure. Some species of *Phaselous* have a specific protein called phytohemagglutinin (PHA) that is toxic in large quantities but is eliminated in the cooking process, especially with the addition of ash.

Magical properties: It may surprise you to learn the magical association of beans with the dead. Beans were served, along with lettuces, at funeral repasts (meals) by the ancient Greeks, and the Romans cast beans into the fire at Lemuria, an annual celebration of the dead. Beans are also associated with fertility goddesses and fruition and can be carried as an amulet for protection. They have long been used in various oracular and divinatory practices.

The Lore

Perhaps besides Cinderella's pumpkin, over the last two hundred or so years, there is one plant that dominates the cult of fairy tales: the bean. More specifically, the beanstalk, as in *Jack and the Beanstalk*. In this story an impoverished widow sends her only son to market to sell their last cow, but Jack instead trades the cow for some magic beans. In some versions, Jack meets an old man on the road, a magician in disguise, who sells him the beans. In a less common version published in Andrew Lang's *The Red Fairy Book* with a note in the preface that states "Lady Frances Balfour has kindly copied an old version of *Jack and the Beanstalk*"—rather than meet a wizardly figure, Jack encounters a butcher who tricks him into trading the cow for the beans.

> *Jack liked going to market to sell the cow very much; but as he was on the way, he met a butcher who had some beautiful beans in his hand. Jack stopped to look at them, and the butcher told the boy that they were of great value, and persuaded the silly lad to sell the cow for these beans.*

Jack's mother was quite dismayed that all he got were a few beans. Jack felt badly but woke up early the next day and headed out into the garden.

> *"At least," he thought, "I will sow the wonderful beans. Mother says that they are just common scarlet-runners, and nothing else; but I may as well sow them."*

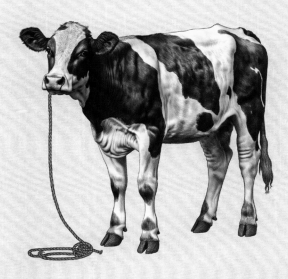

If you've ever planted scarlet runner beans, then you already know how fast they "run" all over the garden, blooming gorgeous red flowers that give way to long bean pods. Inside the pods are the beautiful beans in varying shades from white to black to red to purple, many with mottling of deep purple, quite like little gems. One seed company, Renee's Garden, even sells a variety called Magic Beans. It's easy enough to imagine them twisting their way straight up to the cloud. What young child could resist climbing a stalk that pierces the cloud line, to see what might be up so high? Jack does and finds himself in a beautiful kingdom where he is able to nip bags of gold, a golden harp, and a goose that lays golden eggs from a loathsome giant.

Scarlet runner beans are native to Mexico, Guatemala, Honduras, Nicaragua, and Panamá and were introduced to Europe by John Tradescant the Younger—a botanist, world traveler, and gardener to Queen Henrietta Maria—who brought them back from one of his horticultural expeditions in the early part of the 17th century. Lang's *The Red Fairy Book* was published in 1890, and as per his note, the story had already existed long enough in popular culture to have more than one version.

Scarlet runner beans were first domesticated in Mexico circa 2500 BCE, though there is archeological evidence of the wild form that goes back 7000. The tepary bean (*P. acutifolius*) is native to the American Southwest and Mexico, and is an important crop culturally and as a food source. It has adapted to survive the desert climate, enduring long periods of drought and extreme heat. One Dine' (Navajo) story tells of Coyote running with a bag filled with tepary beans. He trips, and the beans scatter, forming the Milky Way. A similar version tells of an impatient Coyote not wanting to wait for the first people to put the stars in the sky, one by one, from the bag, so instead he takes the bag and flings it at the sky.

In the wild, the common bean, *P. vulgaris*, hails from northern Mexico all the way south to Argentina. Beans have been cultivated for thousands of years in the Americas thanks to the advanced agricultural practices from early civilizations including the Maya, Olmec, and Toltec, as well as the Aztec. Further north, beans were cultivated widely. As Enrique Salmon writes in *Iwigara: The Kinship of Plants and People*, "Nearly every Indigenous language in the western hemisphere has a word for beans."

Mashkodesimin, mashkodiisimin, miskodiisimin, and *miskojiimin* are all Anishinaabe (Ojibwe) words for bean.

The essential principle of the Indigenous gardening method known as the Three Sisters is one of harmony and practicality: cornstalks support the wily bean, the beans have somewhere to go and reinforce the corn, while gourds or pumpkins sprawl out to shade the delicate roots of both and help preserve moisture. Beans, as with all legumes, have the ability to take nitrogen from the air and pass it down into their roots, fixing it in the soil for other plants (corn) to thrive on. Another key component of this relationship is the nutrition. These plants not only work in harmony while growing but, when eaten together, become a robust meal full of nutrients and vitamins. Corn is packed with vitamins but lacks amino acids, something beans have in spades. Together they make a complete protein.

In his seminal herbal, Nicholas Culpeper notes that beans are "plants of Venus, and the distilled water of the flower of garden beans is good to clean the face and skin from spots and wrinkles." He also says that the green husk distilled in water can treat kidney stones. Bean flour can be used in poultices to reduce swelling and inflammation around wounds and to treat engorgement or mastitis for nursing mothers.

It's fascinating that the beanstalk has grown so huge in our minds, though in reality the largest (or longest) growing vines require some form of support to grow upright. You will read later about a cabbage stalk that took on very similar characteristics to the magic beanstalk, growing straight up into the heavens themselves.

Cabbage

"The time has come," the Walrus said,
"To talk of many things:
Of shoes—and ships—and sealing-wax—
Of cabbages—and kings."

—Lewis Carroll, "The Walrus and the Carpenter"

Botanical name: *Brassica oleracea*

Native to: Wild cabbage grows in England and France, but the widely cultivated cabbage in most gardens today is native to the Middle East.

Also called: In lore and old botanicals, sometimes called coleworts

Medicinal properties: An anti-inflammatory, cabbage has fiber, potassium, and vitamins C and K. It also lowers blood pressure. Topically, it can treat a wide variety of ailments, including bruises and sprains. An old remedy suggests laying cabbage leaves in the case of clogged milk ducts in a nursing mother (mastitis).

Magical properties: Prosperity, prophesy, blessings, fertility. Bring a fresh cabbage plant to a new home as a blessing and to bring prosperity to the home and garden. In Scotland and parts of Ireland, cabbages are used as a means of divination on Halloween night. Pull the plant from the ground, and the roots will tell you the type of partner you will have. The connection with cabbage and fertility may stem from the old saying that "the baby is in the cabbage patch" or "found in a cabbage patch" as a term of endearment, saying that someone is sweet-faced. Affectionate, perhaps, but an indication that cabbages were associated with fertility and abundance, like the cabbage that will grow just about anywhere. Cabbage stalks were also used for flight and fairy magic.

The Lore

Although not nearly as appealing as the glorious apple, cabbages can appear as transformative foods in folklore and are worthy of at least a brief mention. Hungry fools desperate enough to eat a wayside garden cabbage without permission may soon find themselves shapeshifting into somewhat laughable creatures like the ass or the donkey, such as the version in Andrew Lang's (wife's) version of "The Donkey Cabbage," from *The Yellow Fairy Book*. It's worth noting that Andrew Lang—a Scottish poet, anthropologist, and writer—edited the famous collection of fairy books (*The Yellow Fairy Book*, *The Blue Fairy Book*, and so on), but the retold fairy tales themselves were actually written by his wife, Leonora Blanche Alleyne Lang. He remained widely credited as the author until acknowledging her contributions in the introduction of *The Lilac Fairy Book*. In a later collection, *The Red Romance Book*, he credits her entirely as the author of the stories.

In "The Donkey Cabbage," a hunter—though in other versions of this story, it's a soldier—is walking home, hungry and weary from the long day. He happens upon a garden of nothing but cabbages and vegetables. Though it is not his food of choice, he says:

> *"At a pinch I can eat a salad; it does not taste particularly nice, but it will refresh me." So, he looked about for a good head and ate it, but no sooner had he swallowed a couple of mouthfuls than he felt very strange and found himself wonderfully changed. Four legs began to grow on him, a thick head, and two long ears, and he saw with horror that he had changed into a donkey. But as he was still very hungry and this juicy salad tasted very good to his present nature, he went on eating with a still greater appetite. At last, he got hold of another kind of cabbage, but scarcely had swallowed it when he felt another change, and he once more regained his human form.*

In the story he then manages to use the magical cabbages to trick a lovely maiden and a witch alike, transforming them all into donkeys to teach them lessons. As in the story of the apples, the "cure" to un-donkey oneself is to eat more cabbage.

In a collection of Russian fairy tales translated in 1872, William Ralston Shedden-Ralston (yes, that is his full and proper name), a British scholar who translated hundreds of Russian stories to English, tells a story called "The Fox Physician" in which cabbage takes center stage. In this instance, *ash-hole* refers to the repository of ashes from the fire, not as a slang term for being a jerk, though you'll soon see the fox is quite the ash-hole.

> *There once was an old couple. The old man planted a cabbage-head in the cellar under the floor of his cottage; the old woman planted one in the ash-hole. The old woman's cabbage, in the ash-hole, withered away entirely; but the old man's grew and grew, grew up to the floor. The old man took his hatchet and cut a hole in the floor above the cabbage. The cabbage went on growing again; grew, grew right up to the ceiling. Again, the old man took his hatchet and cut a hole in the ceiling above the cabbage. The cabbage grew and grew, grew right up to the sky. How was the old man to get a look at the head of the cabbage? He began climbing up the cabbage-stalk, climbed and climbed, climbed and climbed, climbed right up to the sky, cut a hole in the sky, and crept through.*

The story takes a rather sad turn, for after this he finds delicious pie, cake, and stew and eats his fill, then slides back down the cabbage stalk and tells his wife. As you recall, her cabbage did not grow, so he tells her to climb into a sack and he will carry her up to this heavenly feast. So he begins to climb, hauling his wife along by holding the sack between his teeth. As they climb, she grows impatient and asks, "Are we there yet?" The sack falls from his mouth when he speaks, and the sack falls down to the earth, and the old man goes tumbling after. When he opens the bag, he discovers nothing but bones, smashed to bits. He is devastated. Along happens a fox, who asks the weeping old man what is wrong. The fox offers to cure the wife by instructing the old man to

> *"heat the bathroom, carry the old woman there along with a bag of oatmeal and a pot of butter, and then stand outside the door; but don't look inside."*

You can guess where it goes from there ... the clever fox makes a pudding of the wife's bones and eats her all up, then runs off, leaving the old man alone in poverty. It may be of interest to gardeners out there that the use of wood ash can help control the common pests that damage cabbages, such as cutworms and cabbage maggots.

Of cabbage and kings, in 1975, Paul Hawken published his book *The Magic of Findhorn* after spending a year living with the people in the community of Findhorn, located in northern Scotland. Findhorn's ability to grow incredible, oversized vegetables was attributed to their work with fairies, devas, and elementals, including one founding member's ongoing encounter with the Elf King and other highly ranked members of the fairy kingdom. Hawken writes, "I had worked with the earth for years and had seen some fantastic feats of horticulture, but none of them matched up to what was being intimated here—a garden growing in the sand and cold, producing sixty-five different vegetables, forty-two herbs, and twenty-one types of fruit. Even if they could be cultivated in that climate, the reports of 42-pound cabbage and 60-pound broccoli plants made it quite unbelievable."

Today Findhorn remains a spiritual community offering retreats and workshops for those seeking to reconnect with nature and decrease their negative impact on the environment.

In his collection *Irish Fairy Legends*, T. Crofton Croker recalls a gardener named Crowley who was thought to be in cahoots with the fairies and was exhausted each day because every night he was taken on a night journey with the Good People on "one of his own cabbage stumps." It is said that a cabbage stalk or stump was a favorite means of transportation for the fairy folk, who would travel on them in the air.

Cabbages, albeit not necessarily 42-pound cabbages, are a more forgiving vegetable to grow in a climate that doesn't experience extreme heat. Along with many of the brassicas, which include broccoli, cauliflower, and Brussels sprouts, cabbages are a cool season crop and can be grown year-round in mild climates or in early spring or fall in climates with hot summers. It should not come as a surprise, then, that cabbage is a food source in many Irish recipes, where the relatively cool and mild year-round temperatures make it a successful crop. Remember that the potato was introduced to Ireland in the late 1500s, so before that, other vegetables such as cabbages and turnips were staples. Many salad greens including radicchio, endive, lettuces, arugula, and kale prefer the cooler seasons to the hot summers and can be grown on a similar schedule to the brassicas.

In a somewhat bizarre collection published in 1839, *Curiosities of Medical Experience*, compiled by J. G. Millingen, MD, MA and "Surgeon to the Forces, Resident Physician of the County of Middlesex Pauper Lunatic Asylum at Hanwell," the author notes that certain saints subsisted on cabbages. He writes that in an effort to outdo St. Julian Sabas's minimal consumption of bread and salt water, St. Macarius of Egypt subsisted on "a few cabbage-leaves every Sunday."

Nicholas Culpeper, in *The Complete Herbal*, remarks that cabbages and the closely related coleworts, which can refer to a number of brassicas including cabbage and kale, have medicinal uses. One dose of boiled cabbage will "open the body," but the second round will "bind the body." He also says that cabbage juice in wine can help one who has been bitten by an adder.

Cabbage is considered a superfood, packed with fiber, plus vitamins C and K. It's also high in potassium, which can help to lower blood pressure. Cabbage contains a high number of anthocyanins, antioxidants that can help combat inflammation. The US Department of Agriculture released a study showing that red cabbage contained thirty-six different anthocyanins. And recent studies have been conducted on the use of crushed cabbage leaves as a topical treatment for bruises, sprains, inflammation, mastitis, and rheumatic pain, something that cabbage has already been used for in folk medicine for centuries. All of this may well be why the ancient Greeks considered cabbage a remedy against intoxication from the "fruit of the Vine," i.e., wine.

In Scotland, young women determine the figure and size of their future husbands by drawing Cabbages, blindfolded, on Hallowe'en.
—Richard Folkard, *Plant Lore, Legends, and Lyrics*

Corn

Farming looks mighty easy when your plow is a pencil and you're a thousand miles from the corn field.

—Dwight D. Eisenhower

Botanical name: *Zea mays*

Native to: North, Central, and South America

Also called: Maize, mahis

Medicinal properties: Corn contains protein; vitamins A, C, and B; antioxidants; and fiber—all essentials for a balanced diet and healthy nutrition. Unprocessed corn is considered a healthy carbohydrate that can aid in digestion, help reduce inflammation, and even lower cholesterol. An important traditional medicine in many cultures is the use of corn silk (*Stigma maydis*) to treat urinary infections, overactive bladder, kidney stones, edema, and bedwetting. Corn silk is made from the stigmas, a yellow thread-like strand from female flowers of maize. It contains iron, potassium, and zinc, among other minerals.

Magical properties: Corn can be used in offerings to ancestors and in spells involving fertility, love, and prosperity. Use cornmeal, corn flour, or cornstarch for a magical floor sweep to bring prosperity into the home. Corn or other large grain crops represent fertility and abundance. Corn husk dollies are often used as magical poppets during harvest season to represent children or other fertility deities.

The Lore

Some twenty years ago on a trip to study plants in the Amazon basin of Peru, I arrived in the coastal city of Lima exhausted from the long day of flight hopping, with another flight ahead of me in the morning. After dropping my backpack at a hostel (it's true, I once traveled with just a small backpack and only one pair of shoes, but those days are long behind me, darling), I made my way to the nearest café. That was the first time I tried *chicha morada*, the Peruvian purple maize drink made from a specific variety of purple corn, *ckolli*, which is grown in the Andes. The mildly sweet, somewhat tart, and delightfully refreshing drink was a far cry from the nightmarish creamed corn of my youth. It was a gentle and delicious reminder of the many, many varieties of corn out there beyond the basic yellow or white.

Corn is indigenous to the Americas, so it is of central importance in many cultures throughout North, Central, and South America. From the Penobscot Corn Mother of the northeastern United States and Canada to the Mayan Maize God Hun Hunahpu to the Uti Hiata, the Zuni Corn Maiden, there are as many unique corn deities as there are Indigenous cultures.

As Enrique Salmon reminds us in his book *Iwigara: The Kinship of Plants and People*, "Corn is the only traditional American Indian food plant that needs humans, planting its seeds, in order to survive." So it is that corn and people are inextricably connected. Salmon points out that corn as we know it was created some nine thousand years ago, a hybridization of *Zea luxurians*, a wild grass. Though there are a few theories in the botanical, archaeobotanical, and palaeobotanical communities about what the *Zea luxurians* was crossed with to create *Zea mays*, the evidence remains that corn has been a significant food crop for thousands of years. *Zea mays* has endless uses . . . and not just the kernels. Corn can be eaten raw or lightly cooked directly off the cob; it also can be used to make soups, stews, mash, bread, tortillas, dumplings, popcorn, cakes, and, of course, drinks.

Chicha morada is said to have medicinal properties. The bright color of the corn signals antioxidants that enhance the plant's anti-inflammatory properties. Purple corn is also thought to reduce the risks of obesity, diabetes, and even certain cancers. According to Salmon, the corn silk can be harvested and made into a decoction to treat urinary tract infections and kidney stones.

In the *Popol Vuh* or *Popol Wuj*, which translates to "Book of the Community" in the K'iche' language, we find the creation stories of the Maya. Working with the Creator, seven deities conspire, and finally succeed, in making humans from yellow and white corn. Central also to the story are the Hero Twins, two brothers who play a ball game at the behest of the gods of the Underworld. When the twins defeat their opponents, they are transformed into the moon and the sun, and their father becomes the Maize God. According to the National Museum of the American Indian and National Museum of the American Latino corn is central to the Maya calendar, with offerings of corn *atole*—a warm, corn beverage—every 260 days to welcome a new time cycle.

In his book *Corn, Cotton, and Chocolate: How the Maya Changed the World*, author James O'Kon describes the remarkable feat that Maya agronomists transformed a native grass, *Teosinte*, into a high-yield crop: maize. He writes, "The transformation of the grass into maize, which we call corn, was the most significant feat of Maya agronomy and arguably the greatest feat of agronomy in history."

In the Indigenous nations that grow corn as a major food crop, cooking it with other plants, especially beans, helps create a complete protein. Additionally, the traditional addition of ash, which creates potassium hydroxide, softens the corn and unleashes the nutritive niacin locked within. It also makes the corn easier to digest. This was a step that colonists, who learned of corn from the Indigenous groups of the Northeast and Southeast—in particular the Iroquois nations and the Cherokee—failed to recognize. As a result, they did not get adequate nutrition, specifically niacin, from the food source.

Back in Europe, once introduced, corn flourished. It was an easy crop to grow, and the foods made from it were filling. Without the valuable unlocking of niacin, however, people were getting full but were becoming vitamin deficient. This led to the outbreak of a disease now known as Pellagra, or niacin deficiency. The characteristics?

Pale skin, mania, sensitivity to sunlight, confusion, and aggression among them. Many researchers believe this condition was mistaken for vampirism and led to the widespread belief and persecution of vampires, witches, and their companions.

Like pumpkins, corn is not a plant indigenous to Europe, yet it appears in many fairy tales and myths. You may see references to Demeter, the Greek goddess of agriculture, as being the goddess of corn. Her Roman counterpart, Ceres, is similarly referred to, as is Thor, the Norse god. One source of confusion is that the word *corn* was commonly used to represent all kinds of grain crops, including barley and wheat. For example, in *The Golden Bough*, Frazer dedicates entire sections to the study of corn as it relates to Demeter and notes images of Persephone sprouting from the earth as corn. But corn is a native plant of the Americas and was not part of the agricultural crops of Europe until post-Columbus. When we see corn referred to in literature, including *The Golden Bough*, the term is being used in a broad sense. This is why, when it comes to corn, the European tales that include corn as a grain crop may have been retold after its introduction, or may refer to a different staple crop entirely. Corn has become a resilient food crop in Europe, especially those areas with more sunshine, but even in the British Isles, it has found some success. As such, corn-as-we-know-it has made its way into British and European folk literature. One such collection is *Folk-Lore and Legends: English* by Charles John Tibbits (remember that corn had been introduced to Europe nearly four centuries before its publication) in which he describes a creature not unlike a faun or a satyr: the follet. Follet are goat-footed or cloven-hooved beings that Tibbits suggests are more mischievous than evil, with a strong association to Robin Goodfellow, aka Puck. Follet are connected to nature and agriculture and can be helpful, if not a little wild.

> Perhaps the giant son of the witch, that had the devil's mark about her (of whom "there is a pretty tale"), that was called Lob-lye-by-the-fire, was a very different personage from Robin Goodfellow, whom, however, he in some respects appears to resemble.

Regardless of the name of this goblin beastie, Puck, Pan, Follet, or Robin, it offers harvesting of the corn as hard labor in exchange for a bowl of cream. Though it could be argued that, in this case, the creature is viewed as more of a nuisance, eating things up and drinking as he pleases, the bartering between humans and fairy creatures is a common theme throughout the folkloric record. A bowl of milk, cakes, and sometimes wine are all that are required to get some helping hands. But be warned: grow lazy or forgetful or, worse still, leave out a sub-par offering, and you'll be met with utter chaos. These creatures can be as destructive as they can be helpful.

Thomas Keightley's 1892 collection *The Fairy Mythology* recounts the following tale from Germany. The story also mentions the invisible cap, a thread seen throughout many fairy stories. Fairies may possess a cloak, a cap, or another means of going invisible.

'Tis not very long since there were Dwarfs at June near Göttingen, who used to go into the fields and steal the sheaves of corn. This they were able to do the more easily by means of a cap they wore, which made them invisible. They did much injury to one man in particular who had a great deal of corn. At length he hit on a plan to catch them. At noon one day he put a rope round the field, and when the Dwarfs went to creep under it, it knocked off their caps. Being now visible, they were caught. They gave him many fair words, promising if he would take away the rope to give him a peck (mette) of money if he came to that same place before sunrise. He agreed, but a friend whom he consulted told him to go not at sunrise but a little before twelve at night, as it was at that hour that the day really began. He did as directed and there he found the Dwarfs, who did not expect him, with the peck of money.

To dream you see fields of corn, or that you are among unthreshed corn, is a very favorable omen; it denotes success in business; to the lover it announces that you will marry, have many children, and become rich and happy.... If you dream you are gathering ripe corn, it is the most fortunate dream you can have.
—A. H. Noe, *The Witches' Dream Book and Fortune Teller*

Garlic

Garlic is divine.

—Anthony Bourdain

Botanical name: *Allium sativum* (cultivated garlic); *Allium ursinum* (wild garlic)

Native to: Culinary garlic is native to south and central Asia and northeastern Iran; wild garlic is native to Europe and Asia. There are Allium species and counterparts in the Americas as well.

Also called: Wild garlic is also called ramsons.

Medicinal properties: Garlic is used to treat infections and inflammation, and has been used for centuries to ward off the germs of common colds and flus. Some evidence suggests garlic can lower cholesterol, plus the risk of gastrointestinal and other cancers.

Magical properties: The reputation for warding off evils, including vampires, lends garlic to protection spells. Garlic is ruled by Mars and, though not used in love spells, is often used as an aphrodisiac. Garlic and related plants such as chives and onions are planted in garden beds to discourage bugs, so they can also be planted in a magical garden to invoke protection. Garlic is also used in healing spells.

The Lore

Rosemary Gladstar, in her book *Medicinal Herbs*, writes, "If I were forced to only have one herb in my kitchen, garlic would be it." For good reason. Garlic is used throughout much of the world as a traditional medicine, treating all manner of common illnesses such as colds and flus and their symptoms. I remember my own mother coaxing us kids to swallow a clove of garlic each week during the winter. Once, she minced up garlic finely, steeped it in warm water, and had me take this intense decoction to cure a sinus infection. Even the US government acknowledges the proven health benefits of garlic, a member of the lily family, specifically the role of garlic supplements in reducing total cholesterol and low-density lipoprotein (LDL) cholesterol. Additionally, intake of garlic and those in the same family, such as onions, leeks, and chives, can lower the risk of gastrointestinal and other cancers. Fire cider, an old-world medicine, is currently taking the world by storm with its curative properties and for warding off evil colds and flu. It's an herbal vinegar that includes a great many cloves of garlic, along with onion, horseradish, honey, ginger, and cayenne steeped for a number of weeks in apple cider vinegar.

Of all the plants associated with grand, ritual celebration, leeks (*Allium ampeloprasum*), a close relative of garlic, may be among the least likely candidates. We think of soup more than we think of knighthood or immortality, but old customs in Wales tell us that leeks are sacred to St. Dewi and are used as emblems in high offices such as the Knights of the Leek.

There is most assuredly one thing that comes to mind when we think of garlic and lore: vampires. Garlic's reputation for warding off evil spirits, including supernatural vampires, is as long-standing as our obsession with vampires themselves. Interestingly, many of the examples in the story of garlic as an antidote to vampirism are not the large cloves woven into wreaths as we see in movies. That is *Allium sativum*, a native to China that grows large cloves and is now widely cultivated throughout. But in a testament to the antiquity of the "cure" for vampires, it's the wild relative, *Allium ursinum*, that makes a more frequent appearance.

The word *garlic* may well come from the Anglo-Saxon word *gar*—a spear—and *le'ac*—a plant, perhaps owing to the spear-like quality of its leaves. William Thomas Fernie, a curious character who also wrote about the occult power of stones, describes garlic in his 1897 collection *Herbal Simples Approved for Modern Uses of Cure*:

> Ramsons, or the Wild Garlic (Allium ursinum), is broad leaved, and grows abundantly on our moist meadow banks, with a strong smell of onions when crushed or bruised. It is perennial, having egg-shaped or lance-like leaves, whilst bearing large, pearly-white blossoms with acute petals. The name is the plural of "Ramse," or "Ram," which signifies strong-smelling, or rank. And the plant is also called "Buck Rams," or "Buck Rampe," in allusion to its spadix or spathe.

This is the very garlic that appears in Bram Stoker's *Dracula*. In this passage Dr. John Seward, who is the head of a nearby asylum, is attending Lucy at her family's home in Hillingham. Lucy has been pale and requiring transfusions, with two curious puncture wounds on her neck. Seward and Van Helsing are old friends, and Seward has asked Van Helsing to attend to Lucy, that they might determine what her ailment is. While visiting her at Hillingham, Seward describes the arrival of a curious bundle of flowers sent to Lucy by Van Helsing:

11 SEPTEMBER

> Lucy had been examining the flowers and smelling them. Now she threw them down, saying, with half-laughter, and half-disgust, "Oh, Professor, I believe you are only putting up a joke on me. Why, these flowers are only common garlic."

To my surprise, Van Helsing rose up and said with all his sternness, his iron jaw set and his bushy eyebrows meeting, "No trifling with me! I never jest! There is grim purpose in all I do; and I warn you that you do not thwart me. Take care, for the sake of others if not for your own."

Then seeing poor Lucy scared, as she might well be, he went on more gently, "Oh, little miss, my dear, do not fear me. I only do for your good; but there is much virtue to you in those so common flowers. See, I place them myself in your room. I make myself the wreath that you are to wear. But hush! No telling to others that make so inquisitive questions. We must obey, and silence is a part of obedience; and obedience is to bring you strong and well into loving arms that wait for you. Now sit still awhile. Come with me, friend John, and you shall help me deck the room with my garlic, which is all the way from Haarlem, where my friend Vanderpool raise herb in his glasshouses all the year. I had to telegraph yesterday, or they would not have been here."

We went into the room, taking the flowers with us. The Professor's actions were certainly odd and not to be found in any pharmacopeia that I ever heard of. First he fastened up the windows and latched them securely; next, taking a handful of the flowers, he rubbed them all over the sashes, as though to ensure that every whiff of air that might get in would be laden with the garlic smell. Then with the wisp he rubbed all over the jamb of the door, above, below, and at each side, and round the fireplace in the same way.

It all seemed grotesque to me, and presently I said, "Well, Professor, I know you always have a reason for what you do, but this certainly puzzles me. It is well we have no sceptic here, or he would say that you were working some spell to keep out an evil spirit."

"Perhaps I am!" he answered quietly as he began to make the wreath which Lucy was to wear round her neck.

We then waited whilst Lucy made her toilet for the night, and when she was in bed he came and himself fixed the wreath of garlic round her neck. The last words he said to her were, "Take care you do not disturb it; and even if the room feel close, do not to-night open the window or the door."

"I promise," said Lucy, "and thank you both a thousand times for all your kindness to me! Oh, what have I done to be blessed with such friends?"

In the following chapter, Lucy then writes:

How good they all are to me. I quite love that dear Dr. Van Helsing. I wonder why he was so anxious about these flowers. He positively frightened me; he was so fierce. And yet he must have been right, for I feel comfort from them already. Somehow, I do not dread being alone to-night, and I can go to sleep without fear. I shall not mind any flapping outside the window. Oh, the terrible struggle that I have had against sleep so often of late; the pain of the sleeplessness, or the pain of the fear of sleep, with such unknown horrors as it has for me! How blessed are some people, whose lives have no fears, no dreads; to whom sleep is a blessing that comes nightly, and brings nothing but sweet dreams. Well, here I am to-night, hoping for sleep, and lying like Ophelia in the play, with "virgin crants and maiden strewments." I never liked garlic before, but to-night it is delightful! There is peace in its smell; I feel sleep coming already. Good night, everybody.

Pumpkin

Neddie seized the bad pumpkin, and dug out his brains,
Till he felt so light-headed and brimful of pains;
Then two eyes, a long nose, and a mouth big and wide,
They cut in a minute, and laid him aside

—Anonymous, "A Naughty Pumpkin's Fate"

Botanical name: *Cucurbita maxima, C. moschata, C. argyrosperma*

Native to: Central America, Mexico, North America

Also called: Cucurbits, calabeza

Medicinal Properties: Throughout the world the pumpkin is used to treat gastrointestinal diseases; aid digestion; and treat intestinal parasites, wounds, heart disease, urinary tract infections, and even cancer. The flowers are used in wound treatment and to treat male infertility. Pumpkin is also used in pet care, treating digestive disorders in dogs and cats, and as an antiparasite.

Magical Properties: From one pumpkin there are hundreds of seeds, so pumpkins can be used in spells for prosperity and fertility. They are carved into lanterns to protect our homes from the tricks of goblins and to guide wayward trick-or-treaters back home. In general, pumpkins are a magical food considered an emblem of abundance, prosperity, and health.

The Lore

From Linus's Great Pumpkin patch to the grinning lanterns gracing our stoops every October, pumpkins seem to possess a magical quality in and of themselves. My love affair with pumpkins began at a very young age. In the back garden, under an enormous lemon tree, my mom planted a few pumpkins. I used to love to linger out there, looking at the fruits growing and imagining what it would be like if I could live in a pumpkin. One day—I must have been around four years old—my mom wrote a story for me. I could choose the plot, she said, and she would write and illustrate it. I asked if I could become small and live in a jack-o'-lantern in the garden. She indeed wrote the story, with my little Fisher Price *Sesame Street* characters like Ernie, Bert, and Mr. Hooper there to keep me company. When I began to miss my family, instead of turning me back into a regular child, she simply shrunk everyone down to size so we could all live happily ever after inside the pumpkin.

Pumpkins are cucurbits, the same plant family as squash and gourds, and are native to the Americas. Pumpkins, in all their glory, are a gift to the world from Indigenous people of the Americas who cultivated and shared their knowledge with colonists and explorers, creating a cult of pumpkin that is now synonymous with fairy tales and pumpkin spice season.

Squash, beans, and corn were considered the Three Sisters, an Indigenous farming practice that has created stable crops for centuries. The principle is that of companion planting: the squash grows along the ground and creates shade for the roots of the corn, allowing it to retain more nutrients and moisture. The beans vine up the corn, supporting it from the wind and gaining support from it.

Pumpkins were introduced to Europe post-contact with European explorers circa 1492. Like the fast-growing vine itself, pumpkins quickly spread around the world. They're relatively easy to grow and a rewarding crop, producing fruits that store well throughout the winter months, making them a staple in cuisine around the world, and in folklore. And there's no doubt that in the lexicon on pumpkin lore, Cinderella springs to mind, as in *The Fairy Tales of Charles Perrault*:

"Well," said her Godmother, "be but a good girl, and I will contrive that thou shalt go." Then she took her into her chamber and said to her, "Run into the garden and bring me a pumpkin."

Cinderella went immediately to gather the finest she could get and brought it to her Godmother, not being able to imagine how this pumpkin could make her go to the ball. Her Godmother scooped out all the inside of it, having left nothing but the rind, which done, she struck it with her wand, and the pumpkin was instantly turned into a fine coach, gilded all over with gold.

In fact, an heirloom pumpkin variety, *C. maxima*, is known as the Cinderella pumpkin. Deeply ridged like those of the fairy tale carriage, it is a variety that was hybridized and was popular in Paris in the 1880s, during the time Charles Perrault was crafting his famous fairy tales.

L. Frank Baum, the author best known for *The Wizard of Oz*, wrote many other books and short stories beyond the one with which we are all now familiar. Among the characters of Oz that didn't make the cut for the screen, at least until the terrifying animated version released in the 1980s, which we'd all prefer to forget, was Jack Pumpkinhead. Before Tim Burton's version of the Pumpkin King grew so tired of the same old thing, Jack Pumpkinhead was gallivanting the Kingdom of Oz.

His form was made of rough sticks fitted together and dressed in ordinary clothes. His head was a pumpkin with a face carved upon it, and was set on top a sharp stake which formed his neck. Jack was active, good-natured and a general favorite; but his pumpkin head was likely to spoil with age, so in order to secure a good supply of heads he grew a big field of pumpkins and lived in the middle of it, his house being a huge pumpkin hollowed out. Whenever he needed a new head he picked a pumpkin, carved a face on it and stuck it upon the stake of his neck, throwing away the old head as of no further use.

Turnip

I love root vegetables: carrots, parsnips, and turnips.

—Julia Child

Botanical name: *Brassica* spp. (see following note)

Native to: Middle and eastern Asia

Also called: Neep, swede

Medicinal properties: Turnips (*Brassica rapa* subsp. *rapa*) are high in lutein, which supports eye health. They are also rich in fiber, calcium, vitamin C, and potassium. The tender greens of this subspecies are often eaten much like kale or other brassicas and are rich in nutrients. Another species, *Brassica napus* subsp. *napus*, are commonly called turnips, except in the US, where they are called rutabagas (see extensive debate later). They are also packed with nutrients, including fiber, potassium, and calcium. The greens of rutabagas are not commonly eaten. Both brassica subspecies are good for the heart, teeth, and bones and have anti-inflammatory and anticancer properties.

Magical properties: Turnips can ward off evil and bring protection to any household. According to an old custom, serving turnips to a would-be suitor whose advances are unwelcome can rid you of them once and for all.

The Lore

You may not realize this, but turnips are controversial. There is great debate over what vegetable is considered a true turnip, as a member of the brassica family, which includes kale and cabbage. In the United States, the root vegetable we commonly call a turnip is *Brassica rapa* subsp. *rapa* and is white with a purple top on the exterior, with white interior flesh. It may surprise you that this is related to bok choy or pok choi—*Brassica rapa* subsp. *chinensis*, as well as *Brassica rapa* subsp. *oleifra*, used as an oil crop.

Another commonly grown relative is *Brassica napus*, which is widely grown for oil and commonly called rapeseed. The subspecies *B. napus* subsp. *napus* produces a purplish-skinned root vegetable with a yellow flesh. This beauty is known as turnip, neep, or swede throughout Scotland, England, Ireland, and much of Canada. In the US, this vegetable is called a rutabaga. Adding to the confusion, in Germany and other parts of Europe, the word *turnip* sometimes refers to what is known more commonly today as kohlrabi (*B. olercea var. gongylodes*).

In Scotland, the neep was introduced during the Agricultural Revolution of the 18th century, which also coincides with a period of time during which folklore, fairy tales, and superstitions were being widely collected and analyzed.

After far too much reading and research on the topic of turnips, I've come to the conclusion that, for folkloric reasons, the *B. napus* subsp. *napus* (aka the neep, aka the rutabaga) is the more likely botanical candidate in stories. For one, this variety tends to grow bigger in general than its pale cousins. Additionally, early images of lanterns depict a warm, yellow glow more likely to come from the yellow-orange flesh of the neep. Not to mention that these are the root vegetables more commonly grown in Ireland, Scotland, and elsewhere in Europe where the included fairy tales originate, so the *B. rapa* subsp. *rapa* were not as commonly grown, though they were sometimes grown as a food crop for livestock. We could argue that, as a "throwaway food," the American-known turnip would be a good candidate for use as a lantern, but we've already gone too far down the turnip rabbit hole, and we've got to stop somewhere and get on with the stories.

The humble turnip may at first seem a root vegetable that takes a backseat to the more popular carrots or beets, but don't let it fool you. The turnip holds secrets. Although today we think of carving pumpkins at Halloween time, the jack-o'-lanterns weren't pumpkins at all. Pumpkins are indigenous to North America and were not introduced into Ireland until the early 1500s. In Ireland, Samhain—the original Halloween—and its rituals date back centuries before this. Among them, carving jack-o'-lanterns from turnips. One of the most famous Irish origin stories of the jack-o'-lanterns is that of Stingy Jack. There are many variations of this tale, so I've taken the liberty of writing my own version inspired by those stories shared with me around the fire or in the pages of a good book.

There was once a fellow who hated to pay for a thing, even though he had plenty of money, so he was known as Stingy Jack. He was walking the road, for he wouldn't bother to buy a horse or cart, when he came upon the Devil, who was walking the other way.

"And where are you off to, Jack?" asked the Devil.

Jack, well sure this was the Devil, said, "Well, I'm off for a drink. Would you care to join me?"

The Devil hastily agreed, but Jack knew the Devil was there to trick him, so he decided to beat him at his own game. "I've heard you can shapeshift into anything, but I don't believe it." said Jack, laying out his bet.

"I can!" said the Devil, who was, of course, very vain.

"Change into a tree then! I bet you can't do that," said Jack.

And the Devil changed right into a tree.

"That must have been an easy one. Change into a rabbit then," said Jack.

And the Devil quickly transformed into a rabbit.

"Hmmm," said Jack. "These are all too easy. Change into a gold coin. I'm sure you can't do that!"

And in an instant the Devil changed into a gold coin, which Jack quickly picked up and put in his pocket, where he also kept a silver cross, which prevented the Devil from turning back. Happily, Jack made his way to the pub, where he had his drink on credit, though the Devil was burning a hole in his pocket. Eventually, Jack freed the Devil on two conditions: he'd leave Jack be for at least one year, and he couldn't claim Jack's soul when he died. The Devil, of course, agreed. In one year and one hour though, the Devil came knocking at Jack's door.

"Remember me?" said the Devil.

"Ah, of course. But I was just on my way out to the orchard to pick some fruit," said Jack.

"That's no matter. I'll walk with you," the Devil generously offered.

And soon enough Jack took the Devil to the finest tree in the orchard, where high up in a branch grew one of the biggest apples.

"That one there," said Jack, "has got to be the most delicious fruit in this whole orchard, but I cannot reach it."

"I must have it!" called the Devil, who was, of course, quite greedy. And in a moment the Devil had sprung into the tree, climbing up to reach the luscious fruit.

Quickly, Jack pulled out his pocketknife and carved a cross and then laughed because the Devil was stuck in the tree. After he'd had a good chuckle, Jack told the Devil he'd let him down if the Devil would agree to not bother him for another ten years, and, as before, had no claim to his soul when Jack died.

Before the ten years were up, Jack died but God was angry at him for cavorting with the Devil and refused to let him into heaven. When he got down to hell, the Devil, as promised, refused him. And so Jack instead was sent out to wander in eternal darkness, a single burning coal inside a carved turnip his only light. As the people saw him wander, they'd say, "There goes old Jack of the lantern."

Turnips, which were a plentiful crop, especially in the fall when the days grew shorter, made an excellent vessel for a lantern. As the darkness encroached, turnip lanterns could be placed outside on doorsteps and in windowsills as a guiding light. On Samhain night, the night when the veil is thinnest and all manner of ghouls and goblins roam about, a jack-o'-lantern serves to ward off the would-be intruders, including, perhaps the Devil and old Stingy Jack himself. Turnips and other large roots could be carved out as a safe means for transporting a blessed coal from the Samhain bonfire to the home hearth, ensuring luck and health during the darkest time of the year.

To dream of being in a turnip field, or that you see this wholesome vegetable, denotes acquisition of riches, and high employments in the state. To the lover, they augur great fidelity and an exceedingly good temper in your sweetheart, and that if you marry you will be very happy, have fine children and thrive in the world.

—A. H. Noe, *The Witches' Dream Book and Fortune Teller*

CHAPTER 3

The Witch's Garden

What Doesn't Kill You Makes Your Heart Grow Stronger

ACONITE • DATURA • DEADLY NIGHTSHADE • FOXGLOVE • HENBANE
MANDRAKE • POISON HEMLOCK •

For Witch It Stands

With little more than a digging stick and a basket, under cloak of darkness, we'll head to the most secret corner of the garden. Here, among the shadows, grow the witch's herbs, an apothecary growing in the ground. These plants are not for the faint of heart, or for the unwise: a fool in this garden can quickly meet his death. Poisonous plants are not merely part of the plotting murderer's tool kit, they are essential to every healer's pantry. That which doesn't kill you will make you grow stronger, and so much of our modern medicine is rooted in plants that in too large of a dose would be toxic but administered "just so" can have powerful restorative effects. Take the common foxglove, *Digitalis purpurea*, rich with deadly toxins. These very toxins, when administered correctly, prevent a heart attack; yet in too large of a dose, these same constituents can invoke one. So, we must take heed in this garden. Do not let your dogs and cats and guinea pigs run afoul here, nor let your children run astray. This is not a garden for gorging or fort building. This is the realm of the witch.

Aconite

A gentleman is simply a patient wolf.

—Lana Turner

Botanical name: *Aconitum* spp.

Native to: Europe, central China, North America, India.

Also called: Monkshood, wolfsbane, wolfbane, aconite, leopard's bane, blue rocket, Devil's helmet, Odin's helmet, Thor's hat, friar's cap, queen of poisons

Of note: More than three hundred species of *Aconitum* are distributed throughout the northern hemisphere. *A. napellus* is native to Europe; *A. carmichaelii* is native to central China; *A. uncinatum* is native to North America; and *A. ferox* is native to India.

Magical properties: Aconite can be used to unleash the inner witch and as a powerful amulet to remove obstacles and shift your life. When you're working with poison plants, there is always a gamble that purging includes something beloved, so this is a "be careful what you wish for" situation. An effective way to work with aconite is by growing it in a protected area of the garden where no pets, children, or unsuspecting guests can come into contact with it. Treat it with reverence, and it will help you obtain psychic and spiritual enlightenment. Aconite is weighty both medicinally and spiritually and for this reason should be handled with the utmost respect and caution.

Medicinal properties: Anti-inflammatory. Nervine. Treats infections, anxiety, fever. *A. uncinatum* has been studied for treating nerve disorders, including neuralgia and sciatica. *A. napellus* has been used to treat measles, fever, cough, and other symptoms. It stops illnesses from progressing and can treat urinary tract infections, croup, and influenza. *A. carmichaelii* has been used in traditional Chinese medicine for thousands of years as a neuralgic, anti-inflammatory, and to ease pain and swelling throughout the body.

The Lore

A shade-loving plant that likes damp soil, aconite adds a lurking quality to any garden. Stamens peer out from behind brilliant purple hoods; it's a plant that cannot hide yet holds secrets. It is often called monkshood for the hooded appearance of the flowers and is likened to that of Benedictine monks. In Norse mythology the little hoods are equated with Odin's helmets or Thor's hat.

One of the origin stories of aconite centers around Cerberus, the fearsome dog belonging to Hades guarding the entrance to the Underworld. Depending on the story, Cerberus can have anywhere from one to fifty heads but is most often depicted having three. He has serpents' heads running along his spine and the tail of a dragon. Heracles brought Cerberus (sometimes referred to as Kerberos) up from the Underworld, but he became confused and disoriented in the bright light and began to foam at the mouth. Where this spittle hit the ground, the deadly aconite plant sprouted. Who can blame Cerberus, really, though? After spending all of your life in the gloomy darkness of the Underworld, no doubt you'd cringe in the sunlight too.

The goddess Hekate also may have played a hand in causing this powerful flower to come to life. The Roman poet Ovid tells the story in this verse from *Metamorphoses*:

Medea, to dispatch a dang'rous heir,

(She knew him) did a pois'nous draught prepare,

Drawn from a drug, long while reserved in store,

For desp'rate uses, from the Scythian shore,

That from the Echydnæan monster's jaws

Derived its origin, and this the cause.

Through a dark cave a craggy passage lies

To ours ascending from the nether skies,

Through which, by strength of hand, Alcides drew

Chained Cerberus, who lagged and restive grew,

With his bleared eyes our brighter day to view.

Thrice he repeated his enormous yell,

With which he scares the ghosts, and startles hell;

At last outrageous (though compelled to yield),

He sheds his foam in fury on the field;

Which, with its own and rankness of the ground,

Produced a weed by sorcerers renowned

The strongest constitution to confound—

Called Aconite, because it can unlock

All bars, and force its passage through a rock.

It is not lost on this lover of werewolves that the plant known as wolfsbane is said to have sprouted from the magical poison vomit of a supernatural canine.

Elliott O'Donnell, an Irish folklorist, writer, and paranormal investigator describes beautifully in his 1912 *Book of Werwolves*, "lycanthropic streams and flowers" that can transform a person into a werewolf, with the antidote often growing nearby. O'Donnell has this to say of *Aconitum anthora*:

> [T]here is a yellow one, of the same shape and size as a snapdragon; and a red one, something similar to an ox-eyed daisy, both of which have the power of metamorphosing the plucker and wearer into a werwolf. Both have the same peculiar vividness of colour, the same thick, sticky sap, and the same sickly, faint odour. They are both natives of Austria-Hungary and the Balkan Peninsula, and are occasionally to be met with in damp, marshy places.

Wolfsbane is a dichotomy. While it was seen as a werewolf antidote, it also contained the very stuff that would induce an animalistic frenzy. The *bane* in the name alludes to the use of this toxin to poison wolves, but it also speaks to the wolf's dark magic—the use of plants in the exacting dose that witches, healers, and shapeshifters held knowledge of. As with the other poison plants, too much aconite will kill you or cause madness, but the right amount will do wonders for the psyche. Aconite was one of the key ingredients listed in the recorded recipes of flying ointments (see the section "Deadly Nightshade" for more juicy details!). Witches rubbed these salves on themselves to take flight into the darkness, enter into the astral plane, and gain the wisdom of the stars.

It could be argued that aconite is one of the deadliest plants on earth. It contains an alkaloid called aconitine. In Chinese medicine, aconite-derived herbal medicine has been used for thousands of years as an anti-inflammatory and anti-arrhythmic, typically from *A. carmichaelii*. It has shown to be effective against heart disease, asthma, abdominal pains, joint pain, and gynecological disorders including dysmenorrhea or irregular menstruation. The use of this powerful herb in medicine involves neutralizing some of the deadly alkaloids while maintaining the effectiveness of the herb, and it is not to be trifled with. One drop too many, though, and you're in a coma . . . or dead.

In her 1887 book *Ancient Legends, Mystic Charms & Superstitions of Ireland*, Lady Wilde—a folklorist, poet, activist, and mother of Oscar Wilde—describes the Tuatha Dé Danann. They are Ireland's supernatural originals who live in the Other World and were driven underground by the Celts (Milesians), thus becoming the Sidhe or fairy folk. She writes:

> *A splendid sight was the cavalcade of the Tuatha-de-Danann knights. Seven-score steeds, each with a jewel on his forehead like a star, and seven-score horsemen, all the sons of kings, in their green mantles fringed with gold, and golden helmets on their head, and golden greaves on their limbs, and each knight having in his hand a golden spear.*

This might easily be a description for the yellow wolfsbane with its golden helmets upon a green mantle, offering another connection between the magic and the mundane.

The aconites, like digitalis, are fine plants which for their beauty have been introduced in gardens, notwithstanding the violence of their poison. They are found in hilly countries. Their blossoms are blue or yellow, helmet-shaped, and grow in an elegant terminal bunch of the finest effect. Their leaves, of a lustrous green, are cut out in radiating sprays. The aconites are very poisonous. The violence of their poison has given them the name of dog's-bane and wolf's-bane. History tells us that formerly arrow-heads and lance-heads were soaked in the juice of the aconites, to poison the wounds made in war and to make them mortal.
— Richard Folkard, *Plant Lore, Legends, and Lyrics*

Datura

Men become accustomed to poison by degrees.

—Victor Hugo

Botanical name: *Datura* spp.

Also called: Jimson weed, Jamestown weed, thorn apple, Devil's trumpet, Momoy (Chumash) Thorny Apple of Peru, Devil's weed, Yerba del Diablo, mad apple, Devil's snare, zombie cucumber, moonflower

Native to: Mexico, Central America, South America, southwestern United States, India, West Indies, Caribbean

Medicinal properties: All species of datura have strong narcotic tropane alkaloids, including scopolamine, atropine, daturine, and stramonine. The alkaloids atropine and scopolamine are used during surgery to help reduce the production of saliva. Atropine is used to treat muscle spasms, scopolamine to treat nausea. Daturine is used to treat various abdominal and digestive issues and has been used to treat symptoms of Parkinson's. It also is used for pain control in combination with opioids, something the ancient Greeks knew about, using datura and other plants like deadly nightshade in combination with opium poppies to create an anesthetic for surgery. Many Indigenous peoples used the pain-relieving medicine in datura. The hallucinogenic alkaloid is meteloidine and is only found in quantity in some species. *D. stramonium* has been used for centuries in Ayurvedic medicine to treat a host of ailments, including asthma. Studies have shown that *D. metel* also has anti-inflammatory properties. The alkaloid stramonine is being explored as a treatment for depression.

Magical properties: As a sacred plant, datura has been used for thousands of years to gain access to the spirit world. Ingestion of datura is not necessary to access its powerful magic, but respect and reverence are. Use datura to help commune with the spirit world and connect with the unseen. Magically, it can be used to find clarity and purpose and to help with transition.

The Lore

One of my earliest childhood memories is the smell of brugmansia at twilight. We lived in the San Francisco Bay Area, a climate well known for turning Angel's Trumpet into heralding trees. The massive ivory bells hung down, emitting an intoxicating scent. We had a little bench swing beneath the shade of the brugmansia, and as a child of four, I was quite content, swinging there with my sister, inhaling that scent.

Brugmansia were originally classified by Carl Linnaeus (the father of modern taxonomy) as datura, as the plants have many common characteristics, including flower formation and the same tropane alkaloids that induce hallucinations. The split between the two species wasn't botany-official until the 1970s, leaving many home gardeners referring to brugmansia as datura to this day.

Datura has been used as a sacred and medicinal plant in cultures around the world, including Asia, Africa, Europe, and North, Central, and South America. Datura is used in rituals to access the spirit world and seek guidance for matters of the head, heart, and health of individuals and society. It is also used in coming-of-age rituals to signify transition from one phase of life to the next. Archaeobotanical evidence shows datura in use for the last three thousand years or longer in the American Southwest and longer in Mexico, along with Central and South America.

Datura is part of the Chumash creation story, where it is personified as an elder woman called Momoy who transformed into the plant after the great flood. She represents a bridge between the spiritual and modern worlds. Its use is reserved for Chumash shamans who may enter into a trance to diagnose disease and commune with the spirit world. Zuni priests use datura in rituals for rain. Datura is also used in Indigenous communities, including Mohave, Zuni, and Yuma, as a dream aid and for protection.

The Zuni believe that datura was once a brother (A'neglakya) and a sister (A'neglakyatsi'tsa) who lived deep in the Underworld. They often visited the outer world, and when they did, they would each fashion a garland of datura flowers around their heads. Then they would go roaming and observing all around the outer world. When they returned home, they would tell their mother everything they had seen and heard.

One day they were in the outer world when they came upon the Divine Ones, who asked them how they were. The brother and sister replied that they were quite happy, for they had gained knowledge that allowed them to see ghosts, put people to sleep, and spot thieves. The Divine Ones decided the siblings knew too much and banished them back to the Underworld. In the spot where they had stood, datura flowers grew. The Divine Ones called the flowers a'ntglakyn after the boy. These flowers grow in white but also tinged with yellow, blue, and red, representing the four cardinal points.

Sixty-seven different tropane alkaloids have been found in *D. stramonium*, also known as Jimson weed or Jamestown weed. The name *Jamestown weed* comes from the mistaken use of datura leaves as salad greens by early colonizers, specifically British soldiers, which caused delirium and illness. The Boston Historical Society has records of a letter written in 1813 by Thomas Jefferson to a Dr. Samuel Brown in which he discusses Jamestown weed, saying that "Every man of firmness carried it constantly in his pocket to anticipate the guillotine. It brings on the sleep of death as quietly as fatigue does the ordinary sleep, without the least struggle or motion."

John Gerarde, in his 1597 illustrated *Herball, or Generall Historie of Plantes*, calls *Datura stramonium* the "Thorny Apple of Peru" and describes it as having a "drowsy and numbing quality, resembling in effects the Mandrake." He also suggests that as a salve it can cure inflammations and burns.

Datura was likely one of the plants that caused visions at the Oracle of Delphi, and may have also been in Circe's arsenal of plants used to intoxicate and enchant. There are at least nine different species of datura, including *D. metel, D. innoxia,*

D. wrightii, and *D. stramonium.* In Haiti and other parts of the Caribbean, *D. stramonium* is called zombie cucumber, owing to the implications of the stupor it can cause upon consumption and the plant's role in the ritual process of zombification. It is one of the key ingredients.

The common name Thorn Apple, sometimes spelled thornapple, is given to datura owing to its thorny flower pods. There is species of wild cucumber, native to North America, that also produces thorny fruits. This plant is in the gourd family and quite edible, but alas, it is also often called the thorn apple. The telltale difference is that one plant grows on a stalk and the other a vine, but if you're in doubt, leave it out.

Deadly Nightshade

No, no, go not to Lethe, neither twist
Wolf's-bane, tight-rooted, for its poisonous wine;
Nor suffer thy pale forehead to be kiss'd
By nightshade, ruby grape of Proserpine

—John Keats, "Ode to Melancholy"

Botanical name: *Atropa belladonna*

Native to: Europe, Asia, northern Africa

Also called: Belladonna, Devil's cherry, banewort, Devil's berries

Medicinal properties: Ingestion of deadly nightshade can cause hallucinations, confusion, irregular and rapid heartbeat, seizures, and death. However, *Atropa belladonna* contains two tropane alkaloids used in modern medicine: atropine and scopolamine. Atropine is used to increase heart rate and, ironically, to treat poisoning. Scopolamine is used to treat nausea and vomiting after surgery. Both alkaloids are used to reduce saliva during surgery. Atropine is also used in eyedrops to dilate the pupils and to treat muscle spasms.

Magical properties: Rituals connecting to the dead, necromancy, everlasting beauty. Use with caution and do not ingest. It is associated with Hekate (Hecate), witchcraft, the witching hour, and is also said to be an aphrodisiac. It can be used to empower witches in their craft and as an offering to Hekate, Circe, or any powerful ancestral witch.

The Lore

I remember my mother's warning not to eat the shiny purple berries of the *Atropa belladonna*—deadly nightshade—that sprouted like a weed in her garden. She refused to pull the plants, declaring them sacred, and chose instead to educate her young daughters not to touch them. Lucky for us, her lesson worked. Those little bell-shaped flowers, which eventually gave way to the petite fruit, imprinted in my memory. To this day, I recognize this deadly plant in an instant, be it wayside or cultivated. Nor I do pull them from my own garden beds. You never know when you might need a little atropine.

In medieval Italy, the *buona donna*—the good woman—was the go-to for potions, ointments, healing, and spells. This woman, a witch by all accounts, often lived in the woods and knew the ways of plant medicine. You could count on her to heal, hex, and help matters of the heart. Deadly nightshade was in her arsenal, and *buona donna* was the original folk name for nightshade. This name evolved into *bella donna*, meaning beautiful woman, during the 1600s and 1700s when Italian women did, indeed, use the herb as a beauty aid. It was said to redden the skin, creating an attractive blush. It was also employed as a mydriatic—a substance that dilates the pupils. The enlarged pupils were considered more striking. Today atropine, derived from *Atropa belladonna*, is still used to dilate pupils for eye exams.

While the herb has an association with healing, witchcraft, and beauty, it is also feared and looked upon as a plant attended by the Devil himself. The plant's namesake is Atropos, one of the Three Fates of Greek mythology. The Fates spin the thread of life, measure the thread of life, and one, Atropos, cuts the thread of life. She is the one who determines somebody's exact moment of death. It makes sense because even just a little dab of *A. belladonna* can indeed cause death—just a few berries will do the trick, making it a dangerous plant to those who do not understand or respect its powers. Nightshade can bring death, seizures, elevated heart rate, and more, but it can also relieve pain when given in combination with other herbs that contain atropine, such as henbane or poison hemlock, something the ancient Greeks also seemed to understand. They used it both as a poison and an anesthetic in combination with henbane, lettuce, and poppies, to induce a stupor before surgical procedures.

Perhaps most famously though, deadly nightshade is one of the key ingredients in a witch's flying ointment. The plants were soaked in fat and applied as an external ointment. This application would not cause death but would cause hallucinations, including the feeling of flying or, perhaps more accurately, those using it in a ritual setting were able to enter a lucid state of astral projection. In Margaret Murray's infamous 1921 *The Witch Cult in Western Europe*, she writes that it was more likely used in a moderate dose, to induce delirium, as too much would cause death. She also suggests that the ointments would only prove effective if rubbed into broken skin. Life in medieval times was rough, and it's likely that daily life led to at least one or two scratches. After all, witches love cats, no?

In *Witch Cult*, Murray includes a few ancient formulas for flying ointment. Personally, I think the baby fat was likely added in by a non-witch for dramatic effect and was then used to justify the demonization of witches.

1. *Parsley, water of aconite, poplar leaves, and soot.*

2. *Water parsnip, sweet flag, cinquefoil, bat's blood, deadly nightshade, and oil.*

3. *Baby's fat, juice of water parsnip, aconite, cinquefoil, deadly nightshade, and soot.*

Witches were said to anoint their skin or slather the ointment on a broomstick, which they would then ride, absorbing the toxic chemicals through the vaginal mucous membrane. (Because no self-respecting witch wears panties when riding a broom.)

The herb induces madness but also puts a person into a spell-like slumber during which the poisoner would have control over the psyche of their victim. This was, of course, in perfect alignment with the widespread misinformation campaign against witches during the 1500s (which has continued throughout the last five-hundred-plus years) that made it clear that people should believe witches are up to no good. However, the concept of a deliberate nightshade-induced stupor was explored in the 1950s, when atropine was used as a "psychiatric treatment" that would essentially induce a temporary coma, with the doctor being able to administer certain "cures." What could possibly go wrong?

The Valkyries were the fierce, winged maidens who swept over the battlefield and chose who would go to Odin's Hall, Valhalla, upon death. The other half would go to the goddess Freja's meadow, Fólkvangr. Belladonna flowers were associated with the Valkyries, perhaps because of their known psychotropic properties and association with the sensation of flying. Or perhaps because the Norse understood the power, and death, held within the plant, powerful as the Valkyries themselves.

In Greek legend Circe was a powerful sorceress, daughter of the sun god Helios and ocean nymph Perse. She was masterful at incantations, spells, and the use of plants and poisons to effect change. Her domain included the use of "wicked poisons," including nightshade, mandrake, and henbane.

In Homer's *Odyssey*, Circe heard the wrong-way sailors clambering toward her peaceful island. Circe preferred the company of wolves and lions and the forest to humankind, so when Odysseus and his party showed up, she wasn't exactly thrilled. After the crew romped around, killing a magnificent stag and feasting upon it, they finally descended upon Circe's home. Odysseus's crew had already encountered a magnitude of inhospitable people—and creatures—so Circe rather kindly opened the door for them. All the gang, save one, Eurylochus, went in and sat down to a feast she'd laid out, with cheese, honey, and barley meal, and a strong Pramnian wine—a wine described as dry and dark. All of this she laced with baneful herbs, deadly nightshade among them. She intended to get them drunk enough that they'd forget from whence they came, and when it seemed they were sufficiently intoxicated, she turned them into swine and closed them away in her pens. That they did not die shows the aptitude for which Circe understood the powers of the plants.

Seeing all of this, Eurylochus headed back to the ship to inform Odysseus of what had happened. As Odysseus was making his way to Circe's, he ran into Hermes, who offered him a potent herb that would ward off the baneful drugs of Circe, a means to ward off her bewitchery. This herb, called Moly, was described as a plant with a root of black and a flower as white as milk. Some believe it to be *Allium nigrum*, Black garlic, or another close relative in the allium family. Today there is a plant called *Allium moly*, commonly called the Lily leek, but it blooms yellow flowers. You'll remember that allium is the family of garlic and onion, well known as protection herbs and both with long-standing reputations, garlic in particular, for warding off evil enchantments. Odysseus entered Circe's home and resisted her enchantments, or at least her drugs. He slept with her, making her promise to do no more mischief to him and to transform his men back to humans, which she did. They stayed a time (a solid year) and eventually set sail again. It is said that Odysseus and Circe had three sons together (he did return to the island at least once after leaving).

During ancient Roman times, Agrippina the Younger was suspected of killing her husband, Emperor Claudius, with the use of one or more tropane alkaloids found in deadly nightshade, though some contend she simply served him a delicious dish of poisoned mushrooms.

Foxglove

Foxglove and nightshade, side by side,
Emblems of punishment and pride

—Sir Walter Scott, "The Lady of the Lake"

Botanical name: *Digitalis* spp.

Native to: Europe, western Mediterranean

Also called: Fairy bells, lady's thimble, goblin's gloves, dead man's bells, folks' glove, fairy glove, lusmore, Lus Mor, fairy cap, fairy's thimble, witch's thimble

Medicinal properties: Digitalis contains cardiac glycosides such as digitoxin and digoxin, used to treat heart failure and heart arrythmia.

Magical properties: Grow a foxglove in your garden to welcome the fairies and their protection, and ward off unwelcome intruders. Foxglove can also be used to connect with the fairy kingdom and learn the wisdom of other plants. It is in the dominion of Venus and so is good for love spells and rituals, especially those that involve empowerment and self-love. To spot a foxglove means you will see your true love that day. Remember that foxglove is a poisonous plant fiercely protected by unseen forces from the other world, so do what thou wilt. These plants are unlucky as cut flowers indoors.

The Lore

Just look upon a *Digitalis purpurea* in full bloom, and you'll quickly see why it has such a strong connection to fairy lore. Look deep into the bells of the flowers, and you'll see an array of colors and patterns, purple mottling, and shades of pink, white, and sometimes near black, in patterns that seem to almost be a hidden language. It is as if the fairies have written secret messages and only the enlightened can decipher them.

The witch's thimble, foxglove, fairy cap—you'll notice this plant has one of the longest lists of common names, many of which are unique to this plant species. These names give us a very clear picture of this plant's powers. Witch's gloves because witches liked to don the little bells on each finger when cavorting in the woods. Witch's thimble used when sewing magical garments. The same could be applied to fairies, using the finger-capping flowers as gloves or thimbles. All of these names seem to fit this flower, which is magic and medicine all at once.

The names *foxglove* and *foxbell* allude to the relationship between fairies and the foxes, and foxes and this plant. Fairies were said to give foxes the secrets of this plant: that they can wear the blossoms to sneak silently into the chicken coop (or your house) to hunt and to ring the little bells to make a sound that only other foxes can hear, warning them if there is a hunter afoot. This tale comes in varying forms and is most prevalent in Norse and Finnish stories. In Finland, foxes are sacred animals. The aurora borealis is called foxfire because it is the sun reflecting off the tails of magical foxes. When the foxglove bends, it is bowing to a passing fairy or other worldly being.

In Ireland this plant is called fairy cap and also lusmore. There is a story called "The Legend of Knockgrafton" about a poor hunchback who always wears a sprig of the fairy cap in his hat and is thus known as Lusmore. Lusmore makes good with the fairies one night, and they cure his burdensome hunchback. A woman comes to Lusmore to find out if she can get the same fairy cure for her son. Lusmore tells her all he knows about meeting with the fairies and singing along with their music in a complementary way. Of course, the woman's son, Jack, is cantankerous, greedy, and impatient and, instead of waiting to hear the fairy song or joining along, interrupts it. Rather than remove Jack's hump, the fairies drag over Lusmore's lost one and add it to Jack's, making Jack's burden twice as heavy as before. And he dies soon after. The moral of the story here is respect the fairy time and rhythm.

In William Withering's 1785 *An Account of the Foxglove*, he describes bruising the herb and using the juice in an ointment to treat "the King's Evill"—an old term for tuberculosis. He also writes:

> *In the year 1775, my opinion was asked concerning a family receipt for the cure of the dropsy. I was told that it had long been kept a secret by an old woman in Shropshire, who had sometimes made cures after the more regular practitioners had failed. I was informed also, that the effects produced were violent vomiting and purging; for the diuretic effects seemed to have been overlooked. This medicine was composed of twenty or more different herbs; but it was not very difficult for one conversant in these subjects, to perceive, that the active herb could be no other than the Foxglove.*

Withering also goes on to describe dozens of cases in which he prescribed digitalis to treat asthma, shortness of breath, edema, dropsy (heart failure), inflammation, ovarian dropsy (ovarian cysts), gout, jaundice, weak pulse, consumption, asthma-induced insanity, swelling of the brain, general insanity, enlarged liver, bladder stones, heart palpitations, paralysis, and a host of other ailments, many brought on by heavy drinking or childbirth. He reported varying degrees of success with the patients. He experimented with using all parts of the plant, especially the leaves and root.

According to records at the University of Oxford, during World War II when drugs (and everything else) were in short supply, Britain established a Vegetable Drugs Committee. This committee worked with the public to grow and harvest foxglove. Home gardeners, women's institutions, Boy Scouts, and Girl Scouts teamed up with doctors and botanists. The plants were then processed to make digitoxin.

Henbane

Hunting from the stack-yard sod,
The stinking henbane's belted pod,
By youth's warm fancies sweetly led,
To christen them his loaves of bread.

—John Clare, "The Shepard's Calendar," 1827

Botanical name: *Hyoscyamus niger*

Native to: Mediterranean, Europe, northern Africa

Also called: Stinking roger, stinking henbane, fetid nightshade, black henbane, hog's bean

Of note: There are at least eleven different species of *Hyoscyamus* in the world, all known as henbanes, and all of which have narcotic properties. Though in some instances the folkloric record may use them interchangeably, the one that makes the most frequent appearance, and has the longest storied history is *H. niger*, or black henbane. Sometimes *H. albus* (white henbane) is described, the most obvious difference being the color of the flowers. Black henbane does not have black flowers, but a pale brownish-colored bloom with a deep purple (black) center.

Medicinal properties: A source of tropane alkaloids like those found in other nightshades (henbane is in the Solanaceae family) that have been used for thousands of years for pain relief, as a treatment for inflammation and nausea, to regulate bodily fluids, and as a muscle relaxant. It was once used to treat toothache, with (horrifyingly) teething necklaces made from it.

Magical properties: Henbane can be used in weather magic, communing with the dead, enhancing psychic abilities, and empowering an understanding of the dark mysteries of witchcraft. It can also be used in love charms, but be wary of its binding, almost irreversible powers.

The Lore

If all of the plants in this chapter were competing for "deadliest plant on earth," henbane has an edge over foxglove and wolfsbane. It can, and will, grow just about anywhere, especially in roadside ditches and right on the edge of your edible crops. It's in the same family (Solanaceae) as deadly nightshade, and both have the ability to thrive without any invitation.

Henbane has similar tropane alkaloids as those found in deadly nightshade and datura, including atropine and scopolamine, which are still in use today to control saliva and fluid buildup in the lungs during surgery. Henbane is also a source of hyoscyamine, which is used to treat hyperactive bladder, motion sickness, nausea, and irritable bowel syndrome. The ancient Greeks used henbane for anesthesia and pain relief, and the ancient Romans used a combination of henbane, opium, and mandrake to create an anesthesia that would be inhaled prior to surgery. Achilles, whose famed wound at the heel took him down, was said to use henbane leaves to staunch the wounds of soldiers at Troy, no doubt making use of its anesthetic, pain-relieving, and anti-inflammatory qualities.

Nicholas Culpeper, the 17th-century herbalist, describes a number of uses for henbane but cautions that these are all external applications, not internal (so don't be fooled by the wine). The leaves boiled in wine or a juice crushed from the leaves or seed can relieve inflammation of the eyes and elsewhere on the body, including the "privities" and women's breasts. Used with vinegar, henbane can be applied to the forehead to relieve headaches. In the case of accidental ingestion, Culpeper advises goat's milk, honeyed wine, "pine kernels" (pine nuts), fennel seed, nettle seed, mustard seed, radish seed, or onions or garlic boiled in wine. Here again we see garlic as an antidote to a form of madness or otherworldly state.

Henbane is sacred to witches and was also one of the key ingredients in flying ointments and other nefarious witches' brews. Witches could dip the stalk into a well to end drought and gain control over the weather. Scholars believe that henbane is the plant referred to in Shakespeare's *Macbeth*, when Banquo asks, "Have we eaten on the insane root that takes the reason prisoner?" though this could easily be argued to be mandrake, given the history of the use of the mandrake root itself as a ritual and talisman (see the "Mandrake" section for more). Other old words for henbane are *insana* and *alterculum*, for causing insanity, a stupor, and anger. Henbane also has a long-standing reputation for necromancy, magical work involving the dead, the word *bane* stemming from the old Germanic word *bana*, that which causes death. Henbane is the name dubbed by the English, owing to the fact that poultry will die soon after eating it. Oddly enough, folk wisdom declares that hogs can eat it without consequence, thus earning it also the name hog's bean. The ancient Greek philosopher Plutarch described the dead being "crowned with chaplets of Henbane" and their tombs decorated with it. Pliny the Elder described henbane as a plant of ill omen, seen scattered on tombs and served at funeral repasts (feasts). Considering how toxic this plant is, it's not a bad assumption. After all, an overdose can result in heart palpitations, hallucinations, coma, and death. This baneful herb may also have been used by the Völva, the Viking witches and seers who also used sacred plants to commune with the spirit world. There is archeological evidence of henbane seeds from early Viking settlements. Henbane beer was made in honor of the Viking god Thor, and in fact, henbane was used as a flavor additive in pilsner-style beers until the Purity Law prohibiting it passed in 1516. In modest doses, it was believed to have an aphrodisiacal quality, but in large doses, it would, of course, cause some pretty erratic drunken behavior.

Renowned ethnobotanist Karsten Fatur has put forth the theory that it was the seeds and leaves of henbane, and not fly agaric (*Amanita mascara*, the poison mushroom), that Vikings consumed to induce the pre-battle frenzied trance of berserker soldiers.

Oliver Madox Heuffer was an English-born playwright and author. In his 1908 collection *The Book of Witches*, he describes a dreamy witch's home, which I transcribe for you here:

> The witch lives by herself in a dingle, a hundred yards beyond the last cottage of the hamlet. The dingle is a wilderness of brushwood, through which a twisted pathway leads to the witch's door. Matted branches overhang her roof-tree, and even when the moon, breaking for a moment from its net of cloud, sends down a brighter ray than ordinary, it does but emphasize the secretiveness of the ancient moss-grown thatch and the ill-omened plants, henbane, purple nightshade, or white bryony, that cluster round the walls.

From Culpeper to Cunningham, henbane has long been considered an herb associated with Saturn, the god of time. And to Culpeper, this is not necessarily to the plant's credit. (In case you were wondering, *Jakes* are toilets.) As he writes:

> All the herbs which delight most to grow in saturnine places, are saturnine herbs. Both Henbane delights most to grow in saturnine places, and whole cart loads of it may be found near the places where they empty the common Jakes, and scarce a ditch to be found without it growing by it. Ergo, it is an herb of Saturn.

Many scholars and poison plant devotees argue that the noxious juice *hebenon*, poured into the ear of Hamlet's father in Shakespeare's play—"Upon my secure hour thy uncle stole/With juice of cursed hebenon in a vial/And in the porches of my ears did pour/The leperous distilment"—is henbane. They include Henry Nicholson Ellacombe in his 1884 book, *The Plant-Lore and Garden-Craft of Shakespeare*. He writes:

It is very possible that Shakespeare had no particular plant in view, but simply referred to any of the many narcotic plants which, when given in excess, would "take the reason prisoner." The critics have suggested many plants—the Hemlock, the Henbane, the Belladonna, the Mandrake, &c., each one strengthening his opinion from coeval writers. In this uncertainty I should incline to the Henbane from the following description by Gerard and Lyte. "This herbe is called . . . of Apuleia-Mania" (Lyte). "Henbane is called . . . of Pythagoras, Zoroaster, and Apuleius, Insana" (Gerard).

In the land of fairy tales, henbane (or one of its woeful cousins) well could have been the cause of Sleeping Beauty's one-hundred-year nap. There are two versions of this fairy tale—sometimes called "Briar Rose," sometimes titled "The Sleeping Beauty in the Woods." The more common story, and the one that made its way into popular culture largely thanks to Walt Disney, tells of a king and queen who, after years of longing for a child, finally have a beautiful baby, the princess Briar (Aurora) Rose. In a grand celebration of her birth, the fairies of the court come forth to bestow their blessings on the baby. But one fairy, usually described as the bad fairy and in some versions depicted wearing all black and riding a broom, was not invited. In her anger (because if you've learned anything by now it's not to cross the fairies), instead of a blessing, she bestows a curse: that the girl, on the eve of her sixteenth birthday, will prick her finger on a spinning wheel and die. A fairy who has not yet given her gift cannot undo the cursed gift entirely but makes it so that, rather than die, the princess will sleep for one hundred years. In a revised edition of Samber's translation from Charles Perrault, we read

The old Fairy's turn coming next, with a head shaking more with spite than age, she said, that the Princess should have her hand pierced with a spindle, and die of the wound. This terrible gift made the whole company tremble, and everybody fell a-crying.

At this very instant the young Fairy came out from behind the hangings, and spake these words aloud:

"Be reassured, O King and Queen; your daughter shall not die of this disaster: it is true, I have no power to undo entirely what my elder has done. The Princess shall indeed pierce her hand with a spindle; but instead of dying, she shall only fall into a profound sleep, which shall last a hundred years; at the expiration of which a king's son shall come and awake her."

To further prevent this horrible prophecy from coming true, the king orders all of the spinning wheels in the country destroyed. But, of course, one wheel survives. Most versions tell of an innocent woman, oblivious to the prophecy and the ban on spinning wheels, sitting in a room in a high tower of the castle spinning away. Aurora finds her one day, of course, on the eve of her sixteenth birthday. I'd argue that this woman is actually the so-called bad fairy in disguise, and with her, she carries a death draught easily concocted by a cunning witch to put a young girl into a stupor. The girl, who has never seen a spinning wheel in her life, touches it with curiosity, pricks her finger on it, and drops into a sleep-like trance. Could it not be that this spindle was poisoned with henbane, hemlock, or another powerful potion made of it and its narcotic cousins?

In a different version of the tale, touching the spinning wheel lodges a seed beneath the princess's fingernail, causing her to drop into the same stupor. Though in more than one translation this is described as a flax seed, henbane is a wayside herb, growing in ditches along the edges of fields. An errant henbane seed or hemlock seed might just do the trick to knock out the princess.

It's also worth noting here that the versions differ quite a bit from here on out. Both do have the princess in a sleep, and the good fairies come and with their wands put all of the castle inhabitants to sleep as well. This could also easily be a magical potion designed to keep everyone in a trance. In both versions, the beautiful princess is asleep for one hundred years, and a prince cuts through the brambles and woods that grow up around the castle to discover her. In one version, his nonconsensual kiss awakens her. In the other, he sleeps with her (without her consent, and more than once), impregnating her. She gives birth to two babies, and one of them suckles on her finger, until the seed is dislodged, and the princess awakens. Both versions are problematic from a consent point of view, but such is the nature of fairy tales in a patriarchy.

In Piedmont [Italy], there is tradition that if a hare be sprinkled with Henbane juice, all the hares in the neighborhood will run away. They also have a saying, when a mad dog dies, that he has tasted Henbane.
—Richard Folkard, *Plant Lore, Legends, and Lyrics*

Mandrake

And shrieks like Mandrakes, torn out of the earth,
That living mortals, hearing them, ran mad.

—William Shakespeare, *Romeo and Juliet*

Botanical name: *Mandragora officinarum*

Native to: Southern Europe and the Mediterranean

Also called: Official mandrake, mannikin, Circeium, gallows herb, Satan's apple, Satan's fruit, Devil's apple, mayapple

Of note: Another variety, *Mandragora autumnalis*, is very similar to *M. officinarum*: it also forms a man-like root and holds the same medicinal and magical properties. Like its name indicates, it blooms in the autumn instead of the spring and prefers slightly different growing conditions. For the most part, these two varieties seem to be used interchangeably in stories as well as in folk medicine; however, in many accounts the darker root of *M. officinarum* was considered male and the whiter root of *M. autumnalis* the female root. Both are native to Europe, in particular southern Europe. Official mandrake also grows widely in the Mediterranean and is commonly believed to be the one referenced in the Bible, among other works.

Medicinal properties: Like deadly nightshade, mandrake contains tropane alkaloids, atropine, and scopolamine. Both are used in medicine today. Atropine is used to increase heart rate and, ironically, to treat poisoning. Scopolamine is used for nausea and vomiting after surgery. Both alkaloids reduce saliva during surgery.

Atropine is used in eyedrops to dilate the pupils and to treat muscle spasms. There is evidence that shows mandrake was used as medicine for centuries. It was combined with other plants such as poppy, henbane, and nightshade to create a stupor to treat ailments or as an anesthetic for surgery.

Magical properties: Mandrake can be used in love potions; spells to invoke lust and desire, dreamwork, astral travel, protection, fertility, and prosperity; to undo locks, and to increase intelligence. It is sacred to Circe, Hekate, and all witches.

The Lore

From the potting sheds of Hogwarts to heady biblical fields, mandrake is arguably one of the plants most steeped in mystery and magic. Even the Latin name—*Mandragora*—invokes secrets, stored in the earth, and buried in the backs of caves. Derived from the medieval Latin *mandragorās*, the name means "little dragon," as if to connote the warning to any who dare consume it: this plant breathes fire. Formerly classified as *Atropa Mandragora*, it is often still found listed under this botanical name. The word *atropa* refers to Atropos—of the three Greek Fates, she was the one who decided what mortals would live or die. (*Atropa belladonna*, aka deadly nightshade, which you read about earlier, gives the same nod to this deadly deity. One of the other names the ancient Greeks used for mandrake was Circeium, after the high witch Circe, who knew the power of the poison plant path, with mandrake, deadly nightshade, henbane, and other poisonous herbs in her domain.

Mandrake is toxic when consumed; however, it has been used for centuries as a powerful medicine: it is a painkiller, sleep-inducer, sedative, and hallucinogen. The Greek physician Dioscorides (CE 40–90) is recorded as having used it to sedate patients and as an anesthetic. In *Romeo and Juliet*, Juliet's "coma-like state"—which leads to all kinds of trouble—is a mandrake-induced potion.

> *Such rank and deadly lustre dwells,*
> *As in those hellish fires that light*
> *The Mandrake's charnel leaves at night.*
> —Thomas Moore, *Lalla Rookh*

It is said that when you pull the mandrake from the ground, it makes a screaming sound so horrible that it drives you to madness. Does it really make this raucous, demonic sound? Not exactly. *Mandragora autumnalis* blooms in the fall, and the root is typically harvested after the flower has gone to fruit. This means, potentially, pulling the roots from hardened winter ground could lead to a "squeaking" sound. I must note here that this is mostly speculation on my part, based loosely on my experience desperately trying to harvest carrots before the first snowfall. What is more likely is that because the mandrake causes hallucinations and even death, the legend of the satanic screeching is more of a cautionary tale: anyone who harvested this powerful root or dared administer it as medicine, or revenge, was surely doomed to hell. In this way, especially within the doctrine of the church, witches and healers were admonished for gathering a plant that could produce such a strong, otherworldly state of intoxication. It is also possible that the wise women themselves declared this myth of the screaming plant: what better way to protect the scant supply and ensure no villager die than to invoke the horrors of demons?

Because mandrake is so toxic, it was (and still is) frequently used as an amulet. The man-like root is believed to be an aphrodisiac and fertility symbol. Even in the Bible, mandrake is harvested and given to Leah to make her fertile again (all the rage in biblical days):

> *Leah went out to meet him. "You must sleep with me," she said. "I have hired you with my son's mandrakes." So, he slept with her that night. (Gen. 30:16)*

While there is clearly more to the story, the implication is that mandrakes act as an aphrodisiac, and that even the smell and appearance of them were enough to get one hot and bothered (and presumably pregnant).

In her 1888 book *Brownies and Bogles*, Louise Imogen Guiney describes a particular type of brownie—a type of domestic fairy-elf who lives with families and either helps diligently or wreaks havoc—from German folklore:

> *The Alraun, a sort of house-imp shorn of all his engaging diligence, was very small, his body being made of a root; he lived in a bottle. If he was thrown away, back he came, persistently as a rubber ball.*

Interestingly, in the Norse tradition, *Alruna* is the name of a Valkyrie—a female warrior who, like Atropos, decides who will live and who will die, and the mandrake is sacred to her. The term *gallows plant* alludes to the idea that mandrake grows where gallows once stood, again indicating the association with death. In German folklore, the name *alruna* was used interchangeably to describe mandrake and witch.

Mandragora contains tropane alkaloids, which are hallucinogenic and hypnotic. All parts of the plant contain these alkaloids: the leaves, roots, and that luscious little fruit that forms after the star-shaped flower fades, the ripe berry that earns this plant the name of the Devil's apple.

Scott Cunningham in his *Encyclopedia of Magical Herbs* tells how to use a mandrake as a protection charm by placing it on a mantel or above a headboard. He wrote that money placed next to a whole mandrake root will double, but as of this writing I have yet to confirm this theory.

Columella, the ancient Roman author of more than a dozen books about Roman agriculture, wrote, "The Mandrakes' flowers, produce, whose root shows half a man, whose juice with madness strikes." Apparently the ancient Romans were very cautious in how they harvested the mandrake. According to Pliny the Elder, a person must stand with the wind at their back and, before digging, make three circles around the plant with the point of a sword. Then, turning to the west, they may dig it up. Many accounts say that the mandrake must be pulled up by tying one end of a rope around the plant and the other to a dog and let the canine uproot it.

During medieval times, charms or poppets were sometimes made from the mandrake root, which seems perfectly suited to them in my opinion. The root has already got the body! Witches would carve a face at the top and leave the natural strings from the root as a beard and hair. This was then wrapped in a little bit of cotton sheet, for endless good luck. It was believed that if a person harvested mandrake successfully and treated it with reverence, the possessor would gain intelligence, be cured of maladies, find hidden treasure, and be able to undo locks, not to mention ward off evil spirits. You can't really lose with a mandrake, unless you consume it, and then you lose your life, or at least your wits.

In J. G. Millingen's obscure 1917 work, *Curiosities of Medical Experience,* he writes of a gruesome way to increase the power of mandrake:
Albertus the Great affirms that the root has a more powerful action when growing under a gibbet, and is brought to greater perfection by the nourishing secretions that drop from the criminal's dangling corpse.

Poison Hemlock

Scale of dragon, tooth of wolf,
Witches' mummy, maw and gulf
Of the ravin'd salt-sea shark,
Root of hemlock digged i' the dark

—William Shakespeare, *Macbeth*

Botanical name: *Conium maculatum*

Native to: Europe

Also called: Spotted cow weed, dead man's oatmeal, bad man's oatmeal, spotted parsley, poison snakeweed, spotted cowbane

Of note: Poison hemlock is frequently called hemlock, but because there is also a North American tree by this name, it can lead to confusion, especially when sifting through stacks of centuries-old stories. Another plant, water hemlock (*Cicuta* spp.), is a close relative and just as deadly. Ancient Romans referred to poison hemlock as cicuta until the mid 1500s, when *Cicuta virosa* became the designated name for water hemlock. To keep things (slightly) less confusing, Linnaeus changed it to *Conium maculatum* in 1736, and we all go by that now. In the old formularies for witches' flying ointment, water hemlock was often referred to as water parsnip.

Medicinal properties: Hemlock has been used in medicine for its sedative and antispasmodic properties since the time of the ancient Greeks. It contains at least eight powerful alkaloids that have been studied for their potential use in modern medicine. They all affect the central nervous system and in minute doses can increase the effects of morphine. There are also currently studies about the anti-inflammatory properties potentially locked within this plant.

Magical properties: Poison hemlock is sacred to all witches, especially Hekate. Use it sparingly and with great caution. It will help you cut to the truth of the matter and reveal those who have betrayed you.

The Lore

"This plant is one of deception," the herbalist told me. We'd stopped along the dusty road we were on near the Pacific Ocean, just north of San Francisco. She was pointing at a plant with a beautiful umbrella of white flowers across the top. It looked a lot like the Queen Anne's lace I'd gathered from these same hills as a child, and without a flower, it could easily be parsnip. It was hemlock, *Conium maculatum*— one of the deadliest plants on earth. But it also looked an awful lot like a few other plants that grow in the area. The tell-tale sign of poison hemlock is the red splotchy mottling along the stem. This is the plant that killed Socrates. Folk wisdom uses this historical fact to help identify it. The herbalist explained that if I thought of the blood-red mottling as the stains of his blood, I would always be able to recognize this plant. Poison hemlock is a biennial that blooms only every other year, so don't rely on its flower to be your guide.

In her book *Wicked Plants*, author Amy Stewart recounts a story of Duncan Gow, a Scottish tailor who, in 1845, died from eating a sandwich that was made with what his children mistook for an edible herb but was, in fact, the leaves of hemlock. Indeed, it is a plant of deception, often mistaken for wild parsley, parsnip, Queen Anne's lace, and others. Especially when hemlock is not in full bloom, it's not a hard mistake to make. But one with deadly consequences.

In the 1917 translation from the French, Jean-Henri Fabre's *The Story Book of Science* offers a lovely description on the differences between hemlock and its relatives.

> *"Hemlock is still more dangerous. Its finely-divided leaves resemble those of chervil and parsley. This resemblance has often occasioned fatal mistakes, all the easier, because the formidable plant grows in the hedges of enclosures and even in our gardens. A plain enough characteristic, however, enables us to distinguish the poisonous weed from the two pot-herbs that resemble it: that is the odor. Rub that tuft of hemlock in your hands, Simon, and smell."*
>
> *"Ouf!" said Simon, "that smells very bad; parsley and chervil have not that horrid odor. When one is warned, no mistake can be made, in my opinion."*
>
> *"Yes, when one is warned; but those who are not take no account of the smell and mistake hemlock for parsley or chervil. It is in order to be warned that you are listening to me this evening."*
>
> *"You are doing us a great service, Maître Paul," said Jean, "by putting us on our guard against these dangerous plants. Every one at home ought to know what you have just taught us, so as not to gather a salad of hemlock instead of chervil."*

In Margaret Murray's *The Witch Cult in Western Europe*, one of the three formulas for flying ointment contains *du persil* (parsley), *de l'eau de l'Aconite* (water of aconite), *des feuilles de Peuple* (poplar leaves), and *et de la suye* (soot). Aconite (aka monkshood or wolfsbane) and deadly nightshade are "two of the three most poisonous plants growing freely in Europe; the third is hemlock, and in all probability 'persil' refers to hemlock and not to the harmless parsley, which it resembles closely."

Remember, too, that witches kept their secret recipes closely guarded, for magical and practical purposes, so while sometimes translations may be inaccurate, the list of true ingredients may have been deliberately shrouded. Botanists have identified the famous ingredients in the witches' cauldron from *Macbeth* as plants, cracking a code that kept everyone (including Shakespeare) out of trouble.

Jackie Johnson, ND, of the Planhigion Herbal Learning Center in Seymour, Wisconsin, compiled this list of most likely candidates for the Green Bay Botanical Gardens:

Eye of newt—mustard seed

Toe of frog—buttercup leaves

Wool of bat—holly or moss

Tongue of dog—hounds' tooth*

Adder's fork—violet

Blind worm's sting—knotweed

Lizard's leg—ivy

Howlet's wing—garlic or maybe ginger (but garlic was more common)

---

* Hounds' tooth (*Cynoglossum officinale*) is also known as hounds' tongue and was once used to treat dog bites.

Ovid's epic poem *Metamorphoses* describes a most terrible encounter when Athamas and his wife Ino encountered the wrath of Saturnia. The daughter of Saturn, she was disrespected by Athamas and in revenge unleashed the horror of one of the Furies, Tisiphone, upon them. Tisiphone descended on them wearing a robe as red as blood, with a serpent for a belt, and a blood-soaked torch to light her way. She cornered them, and as they tried to flee, pulled two writhing, venomous snakes from her hair and threw them at Ino and Athamas. One snake coiled around Ino and the other Athamas, but they didn't bite them; the snakes stunned them with their noxious smoky breath. Then Tisiphone pulled out the vials of liquid poison she always carried with her, made from vile plants: those that sprang forth from Echidna's venom and Cerberus's spit (remember the Aconite origin story?). This she boiled with fresh blood, stirred with a stalk of hemlock, and poured right onto Ino and Athamas. To finish the job, she created a circle of fire around them with her blood torch.

Some of the potent alkaloids in poison hemlock have been found in a variety of other plants in much less deadly doses, including the carnivorous cobra lilies of the Sarracenia family.

CHAPTER 4

Among the Fields and Valleys

Wildflowers, Meadowlands, and Other

Things to Gather

CLOVER • DANDELION • RAMPION • STRAW • THISTLE

Have a Field Day

After inhaling all those intoxicants, it seems like it's time for a breath of fresh air, no? Bridle your horse and make ready for a little jaunt as we head over hill and dale into meadowland. From the lush shamrocks of Ireland's hills to the wild greens at the forest's edge, this is the domain of the herbalist, the naturalist, and the healer. It is also the dominion of the fairy, for they love a pretty glen. Many plants that are considered weeds or "throwaway" plants are rich in medicine and ripe with stories. While an herbalist's apothecary includes plants far beyond those here, there may yet be some surprises among rapunzel's green leaves and the thistle's spiky thorns. Take a deep breath of that sweet harvested meadow hay, and gather some straw to sit on, while I spin you a yarn or two about some of the open-field plants of fairy tales.

Clover

*The sweetness of life lies in usefulness, like honey
deep in the heart of a clover bloom.*

—Laura Ingalls Wilder

Botanical name: *Trifolium* spp.

Native to: Ireland, British Isles, Europe, central Asia, North America

Also called: Shamrock, trefoil, seamair, seamróg, sea móg, shamroge, honeysuckles, wood sorrel

Of note: Within the genus of *Trifolium*, there are more than three hundred species of plants, many of which are called by the common name *clover*. Some of the species native to Ireland include *Trifolium dubium, T. repens,* and *T. pratense.* There are also several *Trifolium* native to the United States, including *T. stoloniferum*, which is endangered.

Medicinal properties: Clovers have been used for centuries, usually in tea form, to treat bronchitis, colds, and coughs. Topically, clover can be used for a host of skin conditions, including psoriasis, bug bites, and more. The trouble is finding clover that has not been treated with pesticides or other chemicals.

Magical properties: Clover protects against curses and evil enchantments and allows you to see threats clearly. It can be used in love and protection spells.

The Lore

Of all the plants in the world, one of the most recognizable is clover. The shamrock has made its way into everything from public buildings to dollar-store St. Patrick's Day decorations. Few plants, save maybe Scotland's thistle, have such a definitive connection to an entire nation's identity. It grows over hill and dale, giving the Emerald Isle its namesake color. The plant's name *Trifolium* or *trefoil* is Latin for three leaves, and it's believed that the name *clover* is a derivation of the Anglo-Saxon word *cloefer*. The word *shamrock* comes from the Irish word *Seamróg*, pronounced sham-rog, sham-rouge, or sham-raug, depending on the dialect.

Common names like clover can become problematic because more than one plant can have the same common name. Though for many people the terms *shamrock* and *clover* are interchangeable, some believe that a shamrock has three leaves but cannot have four—that this is reserved only for the clover. The folkloric record is all over the map, with the likes of W. B. Yeats using the precise term some claim can't be: four-leaf shamrock, *Seamrógna gCeithre* in Irish. To make matters a bit more confusing, the plants sometimes sold in the United States as shamrocks or Irish clover around St. Patrick's Day aren't *Trifolium* at all; they're oxalis. Oxalis can share a common name (sorrel or wood sorrel) with clover as well. The good news is, when we find these plants in folk tales and fairy lore, what they represent is what is key, not whether the storyteller identified the plant by its accepted botanical name. In addition, these Latin names and classifications have changed and can change still as we learn more and more about the powers of plants.

Though the shamrock is associated with all things Irish and St. Patrick in particular, it was around the 17th century when the use of this plant was specifically associated with St. Patrick's Day. At that time, it was worn as an emblem in his honor and placed in a glass at the end of the day of celebration to make a toast in Padraig's honor. Though it certainly is synonymous with the shamrock, Ireland is not the only country with a connection to this plant. Scotland, Wales, and England all share similar beliefs in the powers of the clover, in both three- and four-leafed form. Even the ancient Romans considered this plant to be a sign of protection and luck.

Three is a powerful number in witchcraft and magic. There were three witches in *Macbeth* not by accident. The shamrock symbolizes the holy trinity (the Father, the Son, and the Holy Ghost) as well as Mother Nature (mother, maiden, and crone). A four-leaved clover, *Seamrógna gCeithre*, known to represent luck, love, hope, and faith, has its own power. In *Ireland's Wild Plants,* Niall Mac Coitir writes, "The possessor of such a shamrock was believed to gain a host of supernatural powers. Whoever had it would have luck in gambling and racing, could not be cheated in a bargain or deceived, and witchcraft could have no power over him." But be warned! Keep hold of the clover and keep it to yourself: bragging about it, sharing it, or giving it away to another diminishes its power. It also enables the wearer to see sorcerers, witches, and cunning folk for who they really are.

Folkard recalls a fairy tale from Cornwall showing the powers of the four-leaf clover to reveal the supernatural world to its bearer. A young milk maid was coming back from milking the cows with a bucket so heavy she could barely lift it to her head, as milk maids were wont to do for ease of balance. So she stooped down and grabbed some grass and clover to put on her head to make it easier to balance the heavy pail. No sooner did she touch the clover than she was surrounded by hundreds of little people using the clover flowers to dip into the milk and drink it down. She saw them gather under the just-milked cow and hold up buttercups, foxgloves, and convolvulus flowers to catch the drops of milk from the cow's udder. When the milkmaid made it home, her mother said, "Ah, you must have put a four-leaf clover on your head."

In his 1910 collection of Irish folk stories, *Beside the Fire*, Douglas Hyde tells of a poor widow who used a shamrock to save her child:

One day there was the only son of a poor widow dying from the destructive plague, and she had not a drop of milk to wet his tongue. She went to the court, and they asked her what she was looking for. She told them that the one son she had was dying of the plague and that she had not a drop of milk to wet his tongue.

"Hard is your case," says a lady that was in the court to her. "I will give you milk and healing, and your son will be as well at the end of an hour as ever he was." Then she gave her a tin can, and said: "Go home now, this can will never be empty as long as you or your son is alive, if you keep the secret without telling anybody that you got it here. When you will go home put a morsel of the Mary's shamrock (four-leaved shamrock?) in the milk and give it to your son."

The widow went home. She put a bit of four-leaved shamrock in the milk, and gave it to her son to drink, and he rose up at the end of an hour as well as ever he was. Then the woman went through the villages round about with the can, and there was no one at all to whom she gave a drink that was not healed at the end of an hour.

Four-leaf clovers are emblems of protection. W. B. Yeats writes that the four-leaved clover guards its owner from all *pishogues* (spells). A story comes down from the Scottish Highlands of an Elfin Knight, from Elizabeth Grierson's 1910 collection, *The Scottish Fairy Book*:

There is a lone moor in Scotland, which, in times past, was said to be haunted by an Elfin Knight. This Knight was only seen at rare intervals, once in every seven years or so, but the fear of him lay on all the country round, for every now and then someone would set out to cross the moor and would never be heard of again.

And although men might search every inch of the ground, no trace of him would be found, and with a thrill of horror the searching party would go home again, shaking their heads and whispering to one another that he had fallen into the hands of the dreaded Knight.

So, as a rule, the moor was deserted, for nobody dare pass that way, much less live there; and by and by it became the haunt of all sorts of wild animals, which made their lairs there, as they found that they never were disturbed by mortal huntsmen.

Now in that same region lived two young earls, Earl St. Clair and Earl Gregory, who were such friends that they rode, and hunted, and fought together, if need be.

And as they were both very fond of the chase, Earl Gregory suggested one day that they should go a-hunting on the haunted moor, in spite of the Elfin King.

"I have heard tell, however, that one is safe from any power that the Knight may have if one wearest the Sign of the Blessed Trinity. So let us bind That on our arm and ride forth without fear."

Sir Gregory burst into a loud laugh at these words. "Dost thou think that I am one of the bairns," he said, "first to be frightened by an idle tale, and then to think that a leaf of clover will protect me? No, no, carry that Sign if thou wilt; I will trust to my good bow and arrow."

But Earl St. Clair did not heed his companion's words, for he remembered how his mother had told him, when he was a little lad at her knee that whoso carried the Sign of the Blessed Trinity need never fear any spell that might be thrown over him by Warlock or Witch, Elf or Demon.

So he went out to the meadow and plucked a leaf of clover, which he bound on his arm with a silken scarf; then he mounted his horse and rode with Earl Gregory to the desolate and lonely moorland.

It was not long before they saw another rider on the moor, but only one of them, St. Clair, who was wearing a talisman, could sense that this was the Elfin King. His companion Gregory wanted nothing more than to ride out to meet the horseman. But his friend, St. Clair, declared:

"Why, man, 'tis the Elfin Knight! Canst thou not see that he doth not ride on the solid ground, but flieth through the air, and that, although he rideth on what seemeth a mortal steed, he is really carried by mighty pinions, which cleave the air like those of a bird? Follow him forsooth! It will be an evil day for thee when thou seekest to do that."

But Gregory scoffed at St. Clair's caution:

"Thy mind hath gone mad over this Elfin King. I tell thee he who passed was a goodly Knight, clad in a green vesture, and riding on a great black jennet. And *because I love a gallant horseman, and would fain learn his name and degree, I will follow him till I find him, even if it be at the world's end."*

And off Gregory went, on and on, never quite able to catch up with the Knight. He rode "over and burn, and moss" until he reached a place so desolate and cold that the wind felt like ice and the green grass had turned white with frost. And then, he saw it:

[T]here in front of him, was a sight from which mortal man might well shrink back in awe and dread. For he saw an enormous Ring marked out on the ground, inside of which the grass, instead of being withered and frozen, was lush, and rank, and green, where hundreds of shadowy Elfin figures were dancing, clad in loose transparent robes of dull blue, which seemed to curl and twist round their wearers like snaky wreaths of smoke.

These weird Goblins were shouting and singing as they danced, and waving their arms above their heads, and throwing themselves about on the ground, for all the world as if they had gone mad; and when they saw Earl Gregory halt on his horse just outside the Ring they beckoned to him with their skinny fingers.

"Come hither, come hither," they shouted; "come tread a measure with us, and afterwards we will drink to thee out of our Monarch's loving cup."

And strange as it may seem, the spell that had been cast over the young Earl was so powerful that, in spite of his fear, he felt that he must obey the eldrich summons, and he threw his bridle on his horse's neck and prepared to join them.

One kindly goblin whispered to him not to join them, but Gregory laughed him off too, saying that he had sworn himself to the Green Knight. Remember that warning I mentioned not to eat or drink of anything in the fairy kingdom, lest you be there forever trapped? The same rule that ruined Persephone's chances of leaving the Underworld? Gregory broke it.

He walked through their ranks till he came to the middle of the Circle; and there, seated at a table of red marble, was the Knight whom he had come so far to seek, clad in his grass-green robes. And before him, on the table, stood a wondrous goblet, fashioned from an emerald, and set round the rim with blood-red rubies.

And this cup was filled with heather ale, which foamed up over the brim; and when the Knight saw Sir Gregory, he lifted it from the table, and handed it to him with a stately bow, and Sir Gregory, being very thirsty, drank.

And as he drank he noticed that the ale in the goblet never grew less, but ever foamed up to the edge; and for the first time his heart misgave him, and he wished that he had never set out on this strange adventure.

But, alas! the time for regrets had passed, for already a strange numbness was stealing over his limbs, and a chill pallor was creeping over his face, and before he could utter a single cry for help the goblet dropped from his nerveless fingers, and he fell down before the Elfin King like a dead man.

Luckily for Gregory, his friend St. Clair followed him. St. Clair, who was protected, found his friend trapped in the fairy ring, but he himself was protected by the sacred trefoil. The old goblin who tried to help Gregory whispered to St. Clair that there was one way to undo the enchantment. He must remain motionless until dawn, despite the cold frost:

> *"Then must thou walk slowly nine times round the edge of the enchanted Circle, and after that thou must walk boldly across it to the red marble table where sits the Elfin King. On it thou wilt see an emerald goblet studded with rubies and filled with heather ale. That must thou secure and carry away; but whilst thou art doing so let no word cross thy lips. For this enchanted ground whereon we dance may look solid to mortal eyes, but in reality it is not so. 'Tis but a quaking bog, and under it is a great lake, wherein dwelleth a fearsome Monster, and if thou so much as utter a word while thy foot resteth upon it, thou wilt fall through the bog and perish in the waters beneath."*

Under the protection of the clover, he miraculously completed this task without waking the bog monster, and when it was done, the enchantment on his friend was broken and everything disappeared, leaving just the two earls, exhausted, on solid ground.

Trifoliums by nature are incredibly resilient plants, able to thrive in areas that are poor in nutrients, grow in a variety of conditions, and bounce back from long periods of dormancy. Clovers and micro-clovers are making their way into lawns as an attempt to out-trend the water-guzzling suburban turf lawn. Micro-clovers, which are just miniature versions of *Trifolium*, give a lush, lawn-like appearance with almost no maintenance. Some seed companies are selling a mix of micro-clover and lawn seed. Clover lawns produce blossoms that attract bees and other pollinators, so it's a win-win for gardeners and nature alike. Some species of clover have become "invasive" in the United States. Often this means taking over or interfering with pristine lawns or agricultural crops, but it can also mean competing with native plants for habitat. For this reason, double-check your *Trifolium* species name to try to cultivate those native to your growing zone.

Many Indigenous people in the Americas consider the local species of *Trifolium* as a food and medicine source. The leaves are primarily eaten raw, and the roots boiled. The roots of wild clover, *Trifolium tridentatum Lindl.* and other *Trifolium* species, are an important food for some of the Pacific Northwestern First Nations, and used as food and medicine for the Southwestern Pomo of northern California. As a medicine, a decoction is made of the blossoms and then drunk to reduce vomiting.

Yarrow is a true meadow plant that grows throughout the world and is known in traditional medicine for its healing powers. Yarrow is said to be able to staunch wounds, and there's an easy way to remember this medicine: the plant's botanical names is *Achillea*, named for the warrior Achilles, who was said to use it to treat soldiers' wounds during the Trojan War. Ironically, he died from a cut to the heel, which led him to bleed to death.

Dandelion

Botanical name: *Taraxacum officinale*

Native to: Europe, Asia

Also called: Lion's tooth, heart fever grass

Medicinal properties: Diuretic, tonic, blood cleanser. It detoxifies the liver and the body, improves skin, and is good for the digestion. It also is an anti-inflammatory and is rich in potassium.

Magical properties: Dandelion magic is a sweet magic. It represents resilience, health, and possibility. Symbolically, the dandelion represents the sun and can be found blooming almost year-round in many climates, enduring as the sun does.

The Lore

Once, when I was on an herbal walk with the renowned herbalist Catherine Abby Rich, she was pointing out a particular plant along the wayside when someone interrupted her and asked, "Isn't that just a weed?" Her response was, "Weed just means WE don't know what to do with it." Of all the plants, this may ring truest for the unsung dandelion. Yes, it's invasive. Yes, technically it is considered a weed, at least certainly in the United States where people go to great lengths to rid their otherwise pristine lawns of dandelions, cursing their cheery yellow flowers, cringing at the puffy clouds of seed heads. They'll chop, dig, and spray all manner of horrors just to get it to curl up and die, only to discover more are sprouting just inches away. Yes, I understand it is invasive and threatens agricultural crops in the United States by competing for soil nutrients, since it will grow literally anywhere. I'm hardly suggesting you plant it. The medicinal value of dandelions is one of the highest and most overlooked sources, as it is nothing if it's not prolific. The biggest challenge for those who wish to harvest dandelion is the unknown chemical treatment, especially near large turf fields and estate lawns.

Who among us, as children, didn't pick up a dandelion to make a wish, blowing with all of our might on the downy seeds, watching the potential for our dreams carry into the wind? The humble dandelion is truly the stuff of fairy tales. The seed heads need not be only for children's wishes. You can use the seed heads to convey a message to another by sending thoughts into the little downy seeds, then blowing them away into the direction your loved one lives.

In his story "The Conceited Apple Branch," Hans Christian Andersen writes of a nobleman's carriage passing by a beautiful apple branch in full bloom. The young woman in the carriage admired it as "a most lovely object and the emblem of spring it its most charming aspect." And so the nobleman broke the branch off for her. She shielded the delicate flowers with her silk parasol as they rode home to their nearby castle. There, she placed it in a vase among fresh beech twigs. All the visitors to the castle stopped to admire it and express their pleasure in its beauty. The apple branch proudly took this all in. In fact, the branch began to wax poetic about the nature of mankind.

Some few said nothing, others expressed too much, and the apple branch very soon got to understand that there was as much difference in the characters of human beings as in those of plants and flowers. Some are all for pomp and parade, others have a great deal to do to maintain their own importance, while the rest might be spared without much loss to society.

The branch had a lovely view out the window where it looked upon all of the other plants it could see. (And yes, I can hear your inner botanist cringe at the thought of a branch having its own life away from the tree, but this is, after all, a fairy tale.) In fact, the branch began to feel sorry for all the other plants, who were not admired as much as it.

> *"Poor despised herbs," said the apple branch; "there is really a difference between them and such as I am. How unhappy they must be if they can feel as those in my position do! There is a difference indeed, and so there ought to be, or we should all be equals."*

At this point, the apple branch began to criticize the pathetic "dog flowers" (aka dandelions), which were nothing but common weeds.

> *"Poor despised plants," said the apple bough, "it is not your fault that you are so ugly and that you have such an ugly name, but it is with plants as with men—there must be a difference."*

At this moment, a sunbeam broke through the clouds and shone down on the apple branch and the dandelion alike, kissing them both as equals. Still, the apple branch thought it was better off.

> *"No one ever places it in a nosegay; it is trodden under foot, there are so many of them; and when they run to seed they have flowers like wool, which fly away in little pieces over the roads and cling to the dresses of the people; they are only weeds—but of course there must be weeds. Oh, I am really very thankful that I was not made like one of these flowers."*

Just then a group of children happened along, picked the yellow dandelions, and proceeded to make garlands of flowers as necklaces and crowns for themselves. And then they gathered the ones gone to seed and tried to blow away all the seeds at once.

> *They had been told by their grandmothers that whoever did so would be sure to have new clothes before the end of the year. The despised flower was by this raised to the position of a prophet, or foreteller of events.*

The sunbeam asked the branch if it yet saw the beauty of this humble flower. Begrudgingly, the apple branch agreed it did, indeed, give pleasure, to the likes of children. But surely not any as grand as the fine lords and ladies who admired the apple blossom.

Then an old lady came into the field, and using a knife, she dug around the roots of some of the dandelion plants to take them for a tea, and to bring to the chemist to sell for medicine.

> "But beauty is of higher value than all this," said the apple-tree branch; "only the chosen ones can be admitted into the realms of the beautiful. There is a difference between plants, just as there is a difference between men."

Just then, the young countess who had placed the bough in the vase and her ladies came into the room. Cradled delicately in her hand was a flower of some kind. Carefully, the countess removed the leaves and then the apple branch saw it.

> [T]here appeared the feathery seed crown of the despised yellow dandelion. This was what the lady had so carefully plucked and carried home so safely covered, so that not one of the delicate feathery arrows of which its mist like shape was so lightly formed should flutter away.

"Isn't it beautiful?" the young lady exclaimed. She decided she would paint the beautiful apple branch and the delicate dandelion to forever preserve their beauty. And the sunbeam kissed them both again, and on the flowers of the apple branch, embarrassed by its own vanity, appeared a delicate pink blush.

Like the old woman in the story, herbalists and healers have known the uses of dandelions for centuries, using it to treat for all manner of ailments, medical and magical. In his 1884 book of plant lore, Richard Folkard writes:

Old herbalists had great faith in the Dandelion as a wonderful help to consumptive people. More recently, in the county of Donegal, an old woman skilled in simples has treated her patients for "heart fever," or dyspepsia, as follows:

She measures the sufferer three times round the waist with a ribbon, to the outer edge of which is fastened a green thread.

If the patient be mistaken in supposing himself affected with heart fever, this green thread will remain in its place, but should he really have the disorder, it is found that the green thread has left the edge of the ribbon and lies curled up in the center.

At the third measuring, the simpler prays for a blessing. She next hands the patient nine leaves of "heart fever grass," or Dandelion, gathered by herself, directing him to cut three leaves on three successive mornings.

Richard Folklard calls the dandelion "the rustic oracle: its flowers always open about five a.m. and shut at eight p.m., serving the shepherd for a clock … and the feather seed-tufts his barometer, predicting calm or storm." While the exact time the dandelions open in your yard varies by time of year, it's quite true that the flower heads open in the morning, typically around six or seven a.m. and close again at twilight.

Rampion

There are two tragedies in life. One is to lose your heart's
desire. The other is to gain it.

—George Bernard Shaw

Botanical name: *Campanula rapunculus*

Native to: Europe, northern Africa, western Asia

Also called: Rapunzel, rampion bellflower, ramps

Medicinal properties: Rampion is edible, including both the leaves and the parsnip-like roots. It is an anti-inflammatory and can be used to treat fevers. The leaves are rich in vitamin C, and the roots have been used to help regulate blood sugar.

Magical properties: Rampion is an unsung hero of the meadow and garden alike, and can be used magically to invoke the gentler fairy and nature spirits. It can be added to love spells and the roots carved into amulets to try to get the would-be lover to notice you. It is less powerful and binding than mandrake.

The Lore

When you think of Rapunzel, I'm betting the first thing that comes to mind is a long braid. But did you know that the very name Rapunzel was dubbed by the Grimm Brothers based on a plant? A plant that is pivotal to the entire plot of the story of Rapunzel itself? *Rapunzel* is the German word for a plant called rampion, the plant that a pregnant woman craves so much that she willingly promises away the baby in her womb so she can have some.

> *One day the woman was standing by this window and looking down into the garden, when she saw a bed which was planted with the most beautiful rapunzel, and it looked so fresh and green that she longed for it, and had the greatest desire to eat some.*

Like the maiden in Rapunzel, rampion is beautiful. It grows in clumps of emerald leaves with little flower spikes of star-shaped, pale purple flowers. The leaves are edible and, like all leafy greens, an excellent source of calcium and iron (perhaps this explains the craving? Many women develop anemia while pregnant, which is a low iron count in the blood). Surely, her body was craving the nourishing nutrients of the rampion! The root is also edible and is somewhat radish-like in texture and taste.

Now if you recall, it turns out that the rampion Rapunzel's mother wanted so much? It was growing in a witch's garden. Here is my own version of the story, which stays true to the basics of the Grimm Brothers' original.

Once upon a time there was a man and woman who longed for a child of their own more than anything. They lived next door to a beautiful garden, full of flowers and herbs, but the garden was surrounded by a high wall that no one dared enter because the garden belonged to a witch. The woman could see the garden perfectly from her second-floor window. She was gazing out at the garden one day when she looked upon a bed planted with the richest green rampion (rapunzel) she'd ever seen. She was seized with a desire to eat it, and each day this desire only grew more intense. She pined so deeply for the rapunzel that she became quite pale and miserable. Her husband, in alarm, asked her what the matter was.

"If I can't get some of the rampion from the garden behind our house, to eat, I shall die," she declared.

Alarmed, he vowed to bring her some.

So carefully, just at twilight, he snuck over the garden wall, snatched a handful of rampion, and brought it straight to his wife.

Thrilled, she made herself a salad and devoured it immediately.

But the next day, she longed for even more. So much so that she again begged her husband to go and get her some.

So at twilight, he scaled the garden wall, and just as he reached into the bed of rampion, he heard a voice.

"Who dares steal my rapunzel like a common thief?" asked the witch, quite aghast at this man's bravado. "You will suffer for this," she added for good measure.

"Please," begged the man, "have mercy!" He explained how his wife could see the garden from their window, and when she saw the rampion, she was seized with an insatiable craving. "She said she would die without it!" he told her.

"I see," said the witch, who wondered why the man—or the woman—hadn't just come round the front and asked her for some. "Alright, I have a proposal for you. I will spare you. And you may take as much rapunzel as you like for your wife, but in exchange you must promise me something."

"Anything!" the foolish man agreed too hastily.

"You must give me the child your wife will birth into the world. I will treat it as my own child, and love and care for it."

The man, who thought he'd gotten one over on the witch because he and his wife had tried in vain for years to get pregnant, agreed. He left with a basket overflowing with rampion.

Not many days later, his wife, who was thrilled at the unlimited supply of rampion, began to swell with pregnancy. And in a few months' time she gave birth to a baby girl. The witch appeared at once, named the child Rapunzel, and took her away.

Rapunzel grew into a beautiful child, but when she turned twelve, her witch-mother shut her away into a tower in the woods. The tower had no stairs or even a door, just a little window at the top. When the witch wanted to see her, she cried out, "Rapunzel, Rapunzel! Let down your hair!" and at that the girl would unfurl her hair that she kept in braids, and unleash the long tresses, which the witch would scurry up. This went on for several years while Rapunzel passed her time reading books, learning the language of the forest animals, and singing. So it happened that a prince rode by and heard the sweetest melody. He saw Rapunzel singing in her tower, and he so longed to visit her but could see no door to knock on nor stairs to climb. He couldn't help but return again and again, just to hear Rapunzel's beautiful song.

One day, he was sitting in the forest just far enough away to be out of sight but close enough to still hear her song. Then he heard an old woman call out, "Rapunzel, Rapunzel! Let down your hair!" He watched as Rapunzel undid her braids and let loose her tresses. Then he saw the witch-woman scale right up.

The next day he waited until dark, and after the witch had left, he walked up to the tower and called out, "Rapunzel, Rapunzel! Let down your hair!" The hair curtain came tumbling down, and the prince climbed up.

Rapunzel was quite alarmed to see a strange man at her window, though now that she thought about it, the voice was a little different than the witch's so she might have suspected. In any case, the prince began to speak kindly to her, and only asked her what she was doing there, and did she need help. Rapunzel did not know what to say, she'd been captive for so long, so she asked him if he would come back another evening. And so, after the witch would leave, the prince would sneak over, and Rapunzel would let down her hair, and he would climb up. They spent hours getting to know each other, and one day the prince asked Rapunzel if she would marry him.

"Hmmm . . .," thought Rapunzel. Life with the old witch was all she'd known, but she hadn't always been confined to a tower. And she missed running in the forest and digging in the garden and riding horses. So she agreed, but she had no idea how to escape because she couldn't climb down her own hair, and if he brought a ladder, the witch would surely notice. They resolved that each time the prince came, he would bring her a skein of silk, and over time she would weave a ladder. This went off without a hitch for weeks, until one day Rapunzel absentmindedly remarked that the witch was so much heavier to pull up than the king's son.

At that, the witch grew furious, knowing that he had been visiting her in secret all these months, so she cut off Rapunzel's hair. She took Rapunzel to a desert far beyond the forest, where she left her alone with nothing.

Then the old witch waited for the prince to come by, and when he cried out, "Rapunzel, Rapunzel! Let down your hair!" she dropped down the braids. He cheerfully climbed up, only to see the witch waiting for him. She came at him with the scissors she'd used to chop off Rapunzel's braids, and in fear he leapt from the window, landing in brambles, which scratched out his eyes. Blinded and brokenhearted, he wandered the woods, relying on the kindness of the animals, and eating berries and drinking from the stream. After many years, he wandered to the edge of the forest where there was a desert, the same desert where Rapunzel had been banished to. He heard her singing and walked toward the sound of her voice. When he got close, she saw him, and knew him at once, and was so relieved that she fell upon him and began to weep. Her tears landed in his eyes, and he could once again see. They made their way to his kingdom, where his father was so overjoyed to see him that he too wept. And they lived happily ever after, of course.

I cannot help but wonder if the witch knew the power of the rampion all along and used it to seduce the woman she knew was expecting a child? Though rampion was largely grown as a vegetable crop, it is not without its mystical powers. There is a belief that rampion is a gateway between worlds. In an old Calabrian story, a young girl pulls a rampion up from the earth and finds a staircase that descends into the realm of the fairies. The ancient Greeks used rampion as a funereal vegetable and made offerings of it on golden plates to Apollo. It seems that this humble cousin to the radish is, in fact, an enchanted plant.

Cowslip, or *Primula veris*, possesses the distinct virtue of unlocking every lock and even breaking iron chains. If you find yourself in Transylvania and want to harvest this plant, you must go out at daybreak and creep through the meadow on all fours until you find it. Then you must knife open your left hand and allow the plant's leaf to curl around the wound. This will give you the power to break locks.

Straw

Creativity comes from a conflict of ideas.

—Donatella Versace

Botanical name: *Avena sativa* (oat); *Hordeum vulgare L.* (barley); *Triticum* sp. (wheat); or *Secale cereale* (rye)

Native to: Cultivated worldwide (see the following note)

Also called: *Paja* (Spanish); *paglia* (Italian); *paille* (French); *tuí* (Irish); *szalma* (Hungarian); *canudo* (Portuguese); *connlach* (Scottish Gaelic)

Of note: *Straw* is a general term for the hollow stalks left over after a grain crop harvest, usually oat, wheat, or barley but may be other plants. Essentially, though, it contains no seed. Oatstraw is sometimes harvested before going to seed for its use in herbal medicine.

Medicinal properties: Oatstraw is beloved among herbalists for its soothing external qualities for rashes, itches, bug bites, and psoriasis. Internally, it is used as a tea or tincture as a tonic medicine that supports the immune system and a nervine, so it is useful in treating anxiety.

Magical properties: Straw brings beauty into the world through objects, amulets, dollies, Brigid's crosses, and scarecrows, so it can be used for protection and magical work that involves the rebirth of beauty. Use it in transitory times when you are re-creating yourself or when ingenuity and creative thinking are required.

The Lore

Many years ago, I was sitting in a pub in the town of Dingle, Ireland, when I noticed an elaborate costume made of straw behind the bar. One piece looked like a cloak, but instead of fabric, it had large lengths of straw hanging down amidst colorful ribbons. The top was pointed, also of straw and twigs, and was drawn together at the bottom so that it looked a bit like a head, but there were no eye or mouth holes.

"He's a Wrenboy!" shouted one of the pub-goers, pointing at the bartender, who smiled and explained what that meant to the starry-eyed American girl.

Historically, Wren Day, or St. Stephen's Day, was a day for hunting a wren, a bird believed to be sacred to the Druids and one that connected this world to the world of the dead. Though the bird is no longer hunted on this day, its symbology persists.

Wrenboys don their straw suits and go from house to house, singing festive songs and play-acting stunts such as fighting or other theatrics to entertain. In Dingle each year, there is a parade. The history of the hunt is murky, but there are claims that a wren betrayed St. Stephen and that is why it is hunted, though it seems just as likely that, like many pre-Christian traditions, the wren was demonized for its role of reverence to pagans. If you ask the bartender, he leaned toward the latter.

The hollow stalks left after threshing a field for its grain are exactly why we use the term *straw* for drinking straws. Not to be confused with hay, which is denser and often used to feed animals such as cows, horses, and other grazers, straw is in essence a by-product of a food crop. But it is far from waste. Straw can be woven and plaited into elaborate costumes, rugs, baskets, hats, ornaments, amulets, and mats. In gardens it is spread as mulch to keep weeds at bay and moisture intact, and the name *straw* comes from the old English word *strew*, meaning to spread about. You can use straw to stuff beds and scarecrows, and straw bales have been used to build houses.

And, of course, in the land of fairy tales, straw can be spun into gold.

In the Grimm Brothers' "The Straw, the Coal, and the Bean," an old lady is set to light a fire with straw and coal to cook her pot of beans, and one straw, coal, and bean escape their fate and run away together. In Andersen's "The Fairy Child," common straw becomes an instrument upon which a fairy child plays a haunting melody. Lady Wilde writes that lighting a "wisp of straw" on a Friday and circling it around a baby's head will protect the child from fairies.

One of the most famous stories that involves turning nothing into something is Rumpelstiltskin. I retell it for you here.

There was once a poor miller who had one beautiful daughter who meant more to him than all the riches in the world, or so he thought. The king and his men happened by the mill pond one day, and to impress the king, the miller blurted out that he had a daughter so talented she could spin straw into gold.

"Well," said the king. "That is quite a skill. Bring her to the castle tomorrow so I can see it."

The young woman was brought to the palace and placed into a room that was full of nothing but straw, a spinning wheel, and a reel. And the king, who was actually a very cruel person, said, "Alright, girlie. Get to work and spin all this straw into gold. Tomorrow morning, if it's not done, I shall have you killed." He locked her into the room.

The poor maid was at a loss. There was no way out of the room, and the task was impossible. She began to weep. Just then, the door opened and in came a curious little man. "Hello there. Why are you crying?" he asked politely.

"The king has told me I am to spin all of this straw into gold before morning, or he will have me killed. And I don't know how to do it!" she answered through her tears.

"What will you give me if I do it for you?" asked the little man.

"What about this?" she pulled off her necklace, which was a tiny gold heart on a gold chain.

"Alright," said the man, taking the necklace. He sat down at once and began to work the wheel. Before daybreak all the reels were full of golden thread, and the little man had disappeared.

The king arrived bright and early, looking forward to the inevitable execution of the maiden and was astonished to see the reels were all full of glittering gold thread. Instead of thanking her, he decided to lock her into a bigger room, with even more straw, and command her to spin it all into gold, or he would have her killed.

Again, she was distraught. She had no way out, and she didn't know how to ask the little man for help. Just then, the door opened and in he strode.

"Now, now," he said. "Don't cry. I see the king has given you an even bigger task to complete. What will you give me this time if I do it for you?"

The maiden didn't have much, but she did have a little silver ring. She took it off and offered it to him shyly. He took it, put it in his pocket, and sat down to spin. This time he spun even faster, and he filled up even more reels. Then the little man disappeared.

When the sun rose, the king was there again, eagerly awaiting either another room full of gold or the maiden's demise. Delighted by the sight of so much gold, the king greedily had another room, this time even bigger, filled floor to ceiling with straw.

"Spin this into gold," he declared. "And I'll make you my wife. But if you fail, you won't live to see another sunrise."

Now this was all too much. She was at a loss and began to weep most bitterly. The little man popped into the room just then and said, "Don't cry! I can do this for you, but what will I get in exchange?"

At this the girl began to cry even louder because she had nothing left to give. No jewelry, her clothes were common, and her shoes of wood. "I have nothing!" she cried and began sobbing all over again.

"How's this? I will spin this all into gold for you, and if you are indeed made queen, you must give me your first-born child."

Desperate, and doubtful she'd ever even be queen, she agreed. And so the little man set to work and in no time he'd filled the room with reels of golden thread. In the morning, the little man was gone, and the king came in to see his request had been fulfilled. Thrilled at the sight of all of that gold, he asked the young woman if they could be married right then and there.

Time passed, and a year later, the new queen had a beautiful baby. As she lay there nursing the child, the little man arrived. "Well, give me what you promised!" he demanded. The queen was horrified; she couldn't give up her beautiful baby. She offered him all the riches and jewels of the kingdom: trunks ladened with gold, ruby-encrusted goblets, the whole lot. But he would not be appeased. The queen began to weep again, and the little man took mercy and said to her, rather grumpily, "Fine! I will give you three days. If you can guess my name during that time, you can keep your child. Otherwise, she's mine!"

The queen thought of all the names she could and asked everyone she knew and everyone in the kingdom for names. When the little man came in the next day, he said, "Tell me, o' Queen, what is my name?"

The queen tried all kinds of names. "Is it Jacob?" she asked. He shook his head. Then she tried Ethan and Andy and Phillip. Then Vincent and Aspen. She tried every name she could think of, and the little man just shook his head, did a gleeful little jump, and left.

She cast a wider net. She asked all of the king's men to ride to all the neighboring cities and bring back lists of all of the names of all of the people. So when the little man came the second day, she said, "Is your name Olaf? Or Christopher? Is it Miles? Ben? Is it Jasper? Dave?" And on and on she listed names, but the little man just shook his head, gave her a mischievous grin, and left.

The queen was beginning to despair, and she sent messengers even further afield, to neighboring kingdoms, to bring back all of the names of all of the people, and all of the plants, and all of the animals. That evening one of the messengers came to see the queen and told her that he was riding home and saw a funny little house way up in the mountains. He crept through the woods and saw, in front of the house, a curious little man doing a dance around the fire and singing:

Today I feast, tomorrow I drink,

For nobody can ever think,

I'll be no more; I'll be no less.

For nobody can ever guess

My name is Rumpelstiltskin!

So, on the third morning in came the little man.

"Tell me, O' Queen, what is my name?"

"Hmmm . . .," said the Queen. "Is it Kenneth?"

"Nope!" said the little man, grinning.

"Oh, is it . . . is it . . . Henrik?"

"No!" And his wicked little grin got even wider.

"Is it . . . Rumpelstiltskin?"

At that the little man screamed, "The devil told you that!" as he grew red with fury. He was so angry that he stamped his little feet until he sank one foot into the ground, then the other, and pulled at them so hard he tore himself right in two.

Ergot (*Claviceps purpurea*) is a fungus that grows on rye and other grain crops. When consumed, it can cause hallucinations; pain in the limbs, including an intense burning sensation in the fingers, toes, and other extremities; muscle spasms; convulsions; and vomiting. The Witch Craze, which began in the 1500s in Europe and is responsible for thousands of innocent people being killed in the guise of purging the earth of evil witches, was fueled by accidental ingestion of this fungus. During a time when conversion to the Catholic Church's doctrine was really ramping up, the symptoms of ergot poisoning led people to believe they had been hexed and bewitched. "Good" citizens were reporting conflated accounts of seeing witches (mostly women) fly and cavort with beasts, goblins, and the Devil himself.

Thistle

Some of the most beautiful things worth having in your life
come wrapped in a crown of thorns.

—Shannon L. Alder

Botanical name: See throughout this section.

Native to: Worldwide species distribution

Also called: See throughout this section.

Medicinal properties: *Cirsium* are antifungal and antibacterial, detoxifying, cleansing, diuretic, and anti-inflammatory. Carline thistle, *Carlina vulgaris,* can help heal wounds, is antiseptic, and is also good for urinary disorders such as UTIs and cystitis. Blessed thistle, *Cnicus benedictus,* offers an array of similar health benefits, as do many of the thistles in the world.

Magical properties: All thistles can be used for protection magic. The Scottish thistle, in particular, represents longevity and endurance, so can be invoked before facing difficult situations.

The Lore

If plants that harm are often plants that heal, then the plants that are covered all over in tiny little swords must do wonders. To be considered a thistle, a plant's leaves and sometimes stems are covered in spiny prickles. Most thistles have an urn-shaped flower head, but the color of the flower petals can range from purple to pink to yellow, which then erupt into a downy seedhead. The majority of thistles rely on wind distribution of their seeds. Most, but not all, of the plants considered thistles are in the Asteraceae family but sport different genus and species names, as *thistle* is a common name for a wide number of plants.

Their native habitat ranges from the Highlands of Scotland to the shores of the Pacific. In 1822, Sir Walter Scott chose the Scottish thistle, *Onopordum acanthium*, as the national emblem of Scotland when George IV visited; however, it is an introduced species. Spear thistle (*Cirsium vulgare*) is what many call the "true" Scottish thistle, as it is native to Scotland. This thistle is the most likely candidate for being the one that Mary, Queen of Scots, incorporated into the Great Seal of Scotland. It also appears on coins and is the emblem for one of the highest orders in all of Scotland: the Order of the Thistle. It's believed to have been established sometime in the late 15th century or early 16th century during the reign of James III. According to the official website of the royals in the UK, "The Order of the Thistle is the greatest order of chivalry in Scotland." This order recognizes sixteen knights as well as Scottish men and women who have contributed to Scotland's national way of life either through public service or other acts. The order's motto is *Nemo me impune lacessit*, which translates to "Nobody provokes me with impunity," which sounds exactly like what happens if you mess with a thistle. The knights of the Order of the Thistle participate in a biannual ceremony called the Thistle Service, where they dress in full regalia, including green velvet robes and white-plumed hats, and join a grand procession to the Order of the Thistle in Edinburgh. It is no doubt not by chance that this ceremony takes place every other year in honor of the fact that thistles are biennials (plants that bloom every other year).

Before any of that, though, was the thistle's role in defending Scotland. As the story goes, in the 13th century, a party of invading Norsemen decided to perform a sneak attack at nighttime on the Scottish clansmen. They removed their shoes to approach as silently as they could but stepped on the spiky thistles. Their cries of pain woke the Scotsmen, who defeated the invaders.

The pollen of Mediterranean-native Barnaby's thistle, *Centaurea solstitialis*, was discovered by archaeobotanists at a Neanderthal gravesite. This puts the connection between man and thistle back to at least 60,000 years ago. Blessed thistle, *Cnicus benedictus*, and Carline thistle, *Carlina vulgaris*, are two of the most commonly used thistles in medicine. The sow thistle, *Sonchus oleraceus*, is native throughout Europe and western Asia, and according to Richard Folkard, it possesses a particularly enchanting quality. The sow thistle is considered a gift from Hekate, and when you see one, you can chant "Open sow-thistle" much as you might say "Open sesame." This will reveal any concealed or hidden treasures in the immediate vicinity.

One of my personal favorites is the cobweb thistle, *Cirsium occidentale*, native to the Pacific Coast of California. It spiny leaves have a very pronounced silver pattern, and its downy seeds drape like cobwebs. Similar indigenous species in the Cirsium family include *Cirsium horridulum*, from which the Seminole make blowgun darts.

The Saanich and Cowichan and other Island Salish groups peel the taproots and consume them, raw or cooked. The Saanich believe that the sharpness of the thistle offers protection in driving away negative forces, and the leaves can be placed in the bath to aid in this matter.

Cirsium are antifungal and antibacterial, detoxifying, cleansing, diuretic, and anti-inflammatory. They can be used externally to treat bruises, burns, and bites. Some thistles have mild analgesic qualities, especially in the root.

Wilheim Mannhardt, a German folklorist who studied under Jacob Grimm, collected a particularly curious thistle story from Mecklenburg, Germany. There is a barren spot that marks where a murder took place, and a strange thistle grows there. Each day at high noon this thistle grows human arms, hands, and heads, and when one dozen heads have grown, it vanishes. To look upon this botanical horror can cause illness or paralysis. Maybe that means no one looks for it too hard.

There's an Andersen fairy tale called "What Happened to the Thistle." It starts out describing a beautiful, well-kept garden surrounding a grand old mansion, resplendent with rare trees and plants and flowers. It is much admired by all who visit the mansion, and sometimes people come just to visit the gardens. The thistle is ignored except by a beautiful woman who visits from Scotland and elevates the thistle to its place:

> Near the fence that separated the garden from the meadow stood an immense this-tle. It was an uncommonly large and fine thistle, with several branches spreading out just above the root, and altogether was so strong and full as to make it well worthy of the name "thistle bush."

To dream of being surrounded by Thistles is a lucky omen, portending that the dreamer will be rejoiced by some pleasing intelligence in a short time.
—Richard Folkard, *Plant Lore, Legends, and Lyrics*

CHAPTER 5

The Woods Are Lovely, Dark, and Deep

Trees, Shrubs, and Woodland Dwellers

ASH • BIRCH • ELDER • HAZEL • IVY • JUNIPER • OAK • PINE

Into the Woods

Now that we've lolled about in the sunny fields and meadows, it's time to cinch up our cloak and head into the forest. Though we've gone well beyond the castle walls, there are kings and queens of another kind here. The woodland spirits reign supreme, and they don't take kindly to litter. Keep your wits about you and listen well; you'll hear the creaking birch and the groaning oak, all with stories to tell. In the company of werewolves and witches who dwell deep within, the woods are lovely, but they are also not to be trifled with.

Ash

Philosophy is a root of science. Science is a branch of a philosophical tree.

—Santosh Kalwar

Botanical name: *Fraxinus* spp.

Native to: Northeast Asia; North America; France; China; areas of Pakistan, India, and Afghanistan; England; Scotland; and Ireland

Also called: Mundane ash, mundane tree

Medicinal properties: Nearly all parts of this tree hold medicinal value. It is antiseptic, anti-inflammatory, antibacterial, anticancer, antifungal, antiviral, and antioxidant. It can treat topical wounds, infections, and bruising as well as gout, arthritis, general inflammation, edema, and urinary diseases.

Magical properties: Prosperity, strength, protection. Witches used ash to commune with nature and work with the fairy and elemental spirits. It can also protect from evil, curses, and bad luck. Because of its association with wells, it can be used when traveling over water for protection or in water magic.

The Lore

Yggdrasil, the Norse world tree beneath which the gods assemble, is said to be an ash tree. With branches that spread across the world and into the heavens and embrace all of the cosmos, and roots that penetrate deep into the earth and the Underworld, Yggdrasill is the tree of life . . . and death. Beneath the tree is a horn that can be used to herald the world at end times, or Ragnarök. Norse mythology describes the first human being made from an ash tree. Though some say there is just one well, modern interpretations of the Poetic Edda describe three wells associated with Yggdrasil, among its roots, including one that is held by an above-ground root. To this day, a well near an ash tree is said to be holy.

With more than sixty different species of ash, this tree has played heavily in lore around the world. Greeks and Romans thought the tree was good luck. Cupid used ash for his arrows until he found cypress to be more effective. Ash is said to ward off serpents and evil, and a fire of ash wood or ash leaves can be used for protection. Richard Folkard writes about a belief regarding ash wood and snakes. I'm not sure whether the tale is a commentary on the power of ash or a critique of a protective mother though.

> There exists a popular belief in Cornwall, that no kind of snake is ever found near the "Ashen-tree," and that a branch of the Ash will prevent a snake from coming near a person. There is a legend that a child, who was in the habit of receiving its portion of bread and milk at the cottage door, was found to be in the habit of sharing its food with one of the poisonous adders. The reptile came regularly every morning, and the child, pleased with the beauty of his companion, encouraged the visits. So the babe and the adder thus became close friends. Eventually this became known to the mother (who, being a labourer in the fields, was compelled to leave her child all day), and she found it to be a matter of great difficulty to keep the snake from the child whenever it was left alone. She therefore adopted the precaution of binding an Ashen-twig about its body. The adder no longer came near the

child; but, from that day forward, the poor little one pined away, and eventually died, as all-around said, through grief at having lost the companion by whom it had been fascinated.

The sap of the ash also holds curative and protective properties. Folkard notes an old custom from the Scottish Highlands that a baby's first food is the sap of an ash. If you bury an infant's first nail clippings beneath an ash, the child will be gifted with a beautiful singing voice. There are a number of other customs related to ash and keeping children and adults alike safe with ash branches and ash leaves. Ash and birch are the most common trees used for the sacred Yule log, which is burned to bring on luck and health. Irish author (and mother of Oscar Wilde) Lady Wilde says the ash tree is protection from bewitchment and enchantment, and the branches can be wrapped around cattle's horns and a child's cradle. If you should find yourself witness to a fairy procession, or fall under a fairy spell, drawn to the fairy ring where they cavort, grab an ash branch for protection.

In his book *Scottish Ghost Stories*, author Elliott O'Donnell recounts a ghost story from the turn-of-the-(twentieth)-century where a vengeful ghost takes safe harbor in an ash tree. And though it comes from circa 1900, it sounds as though it could read right out of a page of *Outlander*.

A woman finds herself a little too late in the evening at the Pass of Killiecrankie, a beautiful glen in the Scottish Highlands where a Jacobite battle took place, and which is reputed to be haunted. This woman witnesses the ghosts of a band of Highlanders running across her path, and when she (against her better judgment, of course) follows them, she sees the bodies of dozens of Scottish and British soldiers lying all across the land. At that moment, the specter of a Highlander maiden drops from the ash tree before her and with a wicked grin produces a phantom dagger, which she proceeds to stab into the hearts of the ghostly British soldiers who lie "dying" on the ground.

The association with ash as a harbinger for the dead is not isolated to one place. In London, there was an ash tree known as the Hardy Tree, and it has a strange past. The reason is that, in 1865, the great literary figure Thomas Hardy was hired to oversee a rather gruesome job. The rising King's Cross Station needed room to expand, and the kirkyard (cemetery) was in its way. The graveyard was dismantled, and the occupants reinterred into a mass grave. Dozens of tombstones were piled together with an ash planted at its center: it's said that Hardy wanted to do something that was a monument to those who had been relocated. The roots of the ash grew around the dozens of headstones, making for a morbidly curious site. Unfortunately, the tree collapsed in 2022. This event reopened discussions about its history, and in the process, photos were discovered of the ash tree in 1926 without the headstones. Whether this photo was incorrectly identified or the Hardy involvement was a myth, nonetheless the tree stood wrapping round the monuments to the dead at least one hundred years.

Although mistletoe is commonly associated with oaks, it can also grow on certain species of ash trees. One such mistletoe, *Viscum fraxini*, has been shown to be an effective treatment against colon cancer.

Birch

When I see birches bend to left and right
Across the lines of straighter darker trees,
I like to think some boy's been swinging them.

—Robert Frost, "Birches"

Botanical name: *Betula* spp.

Native to: Northern hemisphere including North America, northern Europe, England, Scotland, Ireland, Russia, China, Himalayas, and Japan

Also called: *Wiigwaas*, white birch; *wiigwaasaatig*, paper birch (Anishinaabe)

beithe (Irish and Scots Gaelic); *björk* or *björken* (Swedish); *birki* (Icelandic); *koivu* or *raippa* (Finnish)

Of note: Birch are found throughout the world in northern climates, though the one that comes to mind most often is the paper birch, which is native to the northern United States.

Medicinal properties: Birch leaves can be used to treat urinary tract infections and cystitis, along with acting as a diuretic, encouraging the body to rid itself of excess water. It can also be used to treat gout, arthritis, and rheumatism. Applied externally, the bark can be used to treat sore muscles. Use the fresh, internal side of peeled bark directly against the skin. Birch sap produces xylitol, a natural sweetener that also fights tooth decay and is a common ingredient in many toothpastes today. The bark also contains something called betulinic acid, which is antimalarial, anti-inflammatory, and has recently been studied with favorable results as an anti-cancer agent, specifically colon cancer.

Magical properties: Although birch is powerful and plentiful, it is a gentle tree and is associated with kindness and sincere love. Use it in invocations and spells for compassion and love. Birch can also be used for protection when traveling over water. Birch branches were once exchanged as a token of affection between young lovers. Birch is frequently still used as the magical Yule log, burned to bring luck. Leshy, the Slavic forest spirit, is usually avoided but can be summoned in a circle made of birch saplings.

The Lore

Wherever birch trees thrive, there are stories. Throughout northern Europe and North America alike, from Finland and Russia to the Great Lakes, the birch forests are sources of paper, housing, fuel, medicine, and magic. Of the eighteen different birches native to the United States, all are used in some capacity for medicine by Indigenous people. *Betula papyrifera* is known as paper birch, and its bark, leaves, and sap are all valuable in treating wounds. The sap is also boiled into syrup, with species such as *Betula lenta* having the sweetest. The bark of birches, but especially the paper birch, is good for making baskets, canoes, and covering structures.

In Finland, birch wood cups are used to dip into the water for the sauna, and birch branches are used for gentle lashing against the skin to increase blood flow. The Finnish sauna is a place not just for health but also for spiritual connection. The sauna is said to be protected by sauna elves or spirits, and regular offerings are made to appease them, including fresh branches of birch. In early Salem, Massachusetts, brooms were made of birch. In Wales, the maypole (Bedwen) was traditionally made of birch.

The connection between birch trees and fairies seems to exist wherever birch trees grow. The eyes on birch bark are said to keep fairies from entering a certain grove, while in the Highlands of Scotland there dwells a solitary fairy called the *Ghillie Dhu* or *Gille Dubh*, who lives in birch forests. He is covered in moss and leaves and generally keeps to himself, though is said to be kind and protective of children. In William Wirt Sikes's *British Goblins*, which is a collection of folk beliefs and fairy stories from Wales, he recounts the story of "Tudur of Llangollen," in which Tudur encounters "a little man in moss breeches with a fiddle under his arm. He was the tiniest wee specimen of humanity imaginable. His coat was made of birch leaves, and he wore upon his head a helmet which consisted of a gorse flower, while his feet were encased in pumps made of beetle's wings." This little man lures Tudur to a fairy circle, where they attempt to enchant him with their music. Miraculously, Tudur resists. Though the description is similar in appearance, the demeanor indicates it's a different fairy altogether.

In the Slavic and Russian fairy tale of Baba Yaga, a young girl's evil stepmother tells her to go to her aunt to get a needle and thread, but the girl knows that the aunt she's talking about is a witch, a Baba Yaga, and entering into Baba Yaga's territory was sure death. The girl goes to her dead mother's sister, a different aunt, and tells her what the stepmother has asked her to do. The auntie advises her this:

> "There is a birch-tree there, niece, which would hit you in the eye—you must tie a ribbon round it; there are doors which would creak and bang—you must pour oil on their hinges; there are dogs which would tear you in pieces—you must throw them these rolls; there is a cat which would scratch your eyes out—you must give it a piece of bacon."

This advice is also reflected in the tradition on festival days for young women in Russia to tie little red ribbons onto newly sprouting birch trees, to encourage the trees to flourish and as a protection spell.

In another Russian fairy tale, the birch tree plays a central role but in a different way altogether. This one, usually called "The Birch Tree and the Fool," tells of a man with three sons—two clever and one who could tell no lies. When their father died, the clever sons divided up his things to sell, but the third son, who was often called a fool, ended up with nothing but a skinny ox. When it was time to go to market to sell their wares, the third son decided to join them and sell his ox. The other brothers laughed at him, that he might sell such a skinny beast, and they left for market. Still, the third brother tied a rope to his ox and started the walk to town. Along the way he had to pass through a forest where there was a very old birch tree. Whenever the wind blew, the tree creaked.

"What is that birch tree creaking about?" he wondered. And then thought, maybe it's bargaining for my ox. So he said out loud to the tree, "If you want to buy it, the price is twenty rubles!"

The birch tree just went on creaking, and the foolish brother thought it was the birch tree bargaining. "Alright," he said to the tree, "I'll give it to you on credit. I'll be back tomorrow to collect." And he tied the ox to the trunk of the tree and headed back home.

When his brothers returned from market, they asked if he'd sold his ox, to which he explained he had, in fact, sold it, but on credit. He would collect tomorrow. The brothers looked doubtful. The next day he got up and headed to the woods to the birch tree to collect his money. The birch tree was there, creaking away, but the ox was gone, devoured by wolves in the night.

"Pay me my money!" the man demanded of the birch tree, which only creaked in response. "Alright," he said in response to the creaking, "I'll give you one day more." And he headed home.

When his brothers saw him, they asked if he'd gotten his money. "No, I am to collect tomorrow." Fearing he'd been taken advantage of, they asked, "Who did you sell your ox to?"

"To the withered old birch in the forest," he explained.

"Ugh," groaned the brothers.

On the morning of the third day, he dressed and headed into the forest. When he arrived at the birch tree, he did not see his ox or his money. The birch tree creaked.

Angry that he had been put off yet again, he grabbed his hatchet and chopped into the tree.

The birch tree was very old, and it had in it a hollow, in which thieves had stashed a pot of gold. When he chopped into the tree, this was revealed. "Aha! I knew you were holding out on me," said the man. He gathered up as much gold as he could carry, then happily headed home.

When he arrived at home, his brothers saw the gold, and their eyes lit up. "Where did you get that?" they asked.

"I got it for my ox," he replied. "And there's more where that came from!"

Now I warn you, reader, here is where the story takes a dark turn. The three brothers went into the woods and retrieved all the money from the birch tree's hollow.

"We must never tell anyone of this gold," said one of the brothers. "For we will be surely robbed if we do."

"Yes," said the other, wise brother. "We should hide it and use it just a little at a time."

"I'll never tell another soul!" declared the foolish brother, who by now wasn't looking quite as foolish in their eyes.

As they made their way home, they encountered a Diachok (a layman worker of the church).

"What are you three brothers hunting in these woods?" asked the Diachok.

"Mushrooms!" said the two brothers in unison, while the third brother called out, "Gold! See?"

The Diachok saw the sack of gold and immediately stuck his hand in to take some. This angered the third brother, who had worked so hard to sell his ox. He took his hatchet and killed the Diachok.

"Oh no!" groaned his brothers, but determined to protect their sibling, they dragged the body home and put it in the cellar. A few days later, people were combing the area looking for the Diachok, so the brothers decided the best move was to

kill a goat, bury it in the basement, then move the Diachok's body, under cover of night, back into the woods to bury it deeply where no one would find it.

A few more days passed and people were looking everywhere, asking for the Diachok. One day, the foolish brother was outside tending his little garden when he heard people calling for the Diachok. He said, "Why do you want him? I killed him days ago, and my brothers put him in the cellar."

Horrified, the people stormed into the house. "Show him to us!" the angry mob cried. The two older brothers jumped up, but the third brother went down into the cellar.

"Did your Diachok have dark hair?" he called from below.

"He did!"

"And bearded?"

"Yes!"

"With two horns?"

Everyone looked confused.

"What are you talking about?" they cried, and even the clever brothers were lost.

"Ah, see for yourselves!" and he hurled the goat head up at them.

The people left the brothers alone after that.

Although we may think papyrus was the first paper, with evidence showing the reedy plant used to make paper as far back as 3000 BCE, birch bark has also been recorded as an early paper. The Vindolanda tablets are some of the oldest surviving documents in Britain, dating back to 100–200 CE, and are made of birch, alder, and oak.

Elder

The wound is the place where the Light enters you.

—Rumi

Botanical name: *Sambucus* spp.

Native to: North America, most of Europe

Also called: Elderberry, elderflower, bour tree

Medicinal properties: Elderberries are flowers used to treat bronchitis, coughs, colds, and other respiratory issues. The flowers can also be used in an infusion to brighten skin, and an ointment made from the leaves or flowers can calm irritated skin and can be used to treat bruises, burns, and sprains.

Magical properties: Elder is known to protect from evil spirits and curses, reveals magical beings to humans, and brings compassion to the user. It is sacred to fairies and fairy magic. Never use any part of elder without express permission from the tree. If you don't know whether permission was asked before harvest, take a pass.

The Lore

Imagine an easy-to-grow tree that doesn't take over, that erupts into hundreds of fragrant white blooms, and produces rich purple berries packed with antioxidants and vitamin C, a tree that nearly every part has healing properties, and it's easy to see why the elder is held in such high regard worldwide for its medicine and its magic.

Elder is inhabited by a dryad-like spirit; some call her Hyldemoer (Elder Mother) or Hylde-qvinde (Elder woman). She dwells within the elder tree and protects its medicine. Picking the flowers, harvesting the berries, or interfering with any part of the elder without explicit permission from the Elder Mother is a huge taboo.

In the book *A Garden of Herbs*, gardener, herbalist, and author Eleanour Sinclair Rohde writes, "However tiny the herb garden, there should be at least one elder in it, for all herbs are under protection of the spirit of the Elder. She is the Elder Mother or Elder woman, who never fails to avenge any injury done to the tree, and when the elder is picked or cut, she must first give her permission."

Hans Christian Andersen no doubt grew up hearing stories about the Elder Mother in his native Denmark. In Andersen's fairy tales, the story is usually called "The Elderbush" or "Elder-Tree Mother" or similar, depending on the translation. The story begins with a little boy who catches a cold owing to "getting his feet wet" while walking to school, which I take to mean jumping in puddles! In any case, he catches a cold, and his mother puts him to bed. She makes him a pot of elder tea. A neighbor, usually described as a jolly or merry old bachelor with no wife or children of his own, is a great storyteller, so he stops in. He sits beside the bed and after a moment tells the boy to look in the teapot, for there is a story in there.

> And as the little boy looked at the tea-pot, the lid rose up gradually, the elder-tree blossoms sprang forth one by one, fresh and white; long boughs came forth, even out of the spout they grew up in all directions, and formed a bush—nay, a large elder tree, which stretched its branches up to the bed and pushed the curtains aside; and there were so many blossoms and such a sweet fragrance! In the midst of the tree sat a kindly-looking old woman with a strange dress; it was as green as the leaves, and trimmed with large white blossoms, so that it was difficult to say if it was real cloth or the leaves and blossoms of the elder tree.

If permission is granted, an elder tree offers countless benefits. Botanically speaking, it's a prolific bloomer, attracting pollinators to the garden, which benefits all crops, especially flowering fruits and food crops.

The berries of the elder, typically made into a syrup, can be used to treat colds, coughs, and fevers. You can find this syrup in drugstores around the world, sometimes sold as Sambucus rather than elderberry. Take heed, though. The unripe berries are actually toxic and should not be consumed in any form. In Russia, the elder twigs were thought to be able to remove toxins and illness from the body, but be careful if you try this cure. You must take the twig and put it in the ground somewhere without saying a word, and the next person to see it will carry the illness. Not the best cure, but we can't change the folkloric record. Similarly, there's a funny old charm where you rub an elder branch across any warts you have and then make a notch in the branch for each wart. Bury the twig, and when it decomposes, so will your warts. A different cure suggests rubbing the fresh shoot of an elder branch on the warts themselves and then burying it. This treatment is wise because elder has antiseptic and antiviral properties.

Elder will protect your garden and home, but it should never be used to build it, or any of its furnishings. Using elder this way is bad luck, and there are countless stories of people waking bruised and pinched in the night because the object made from elder was not made with permission from the Elder woman, and she took revenge.

To seek permission from the elder for use of any of its parts, including berries, bark, flower, wood, or even discarded twigs, make a sincere request of the Elder Mother before touching it. One Danish tradition is to request permission out loud, wait to see if the tree objects, and if not, spit three times before harvesting only what you need.

Standing beneath or near an elder on Midsummer's Eve will allow you to see trolls and fairies as they proceed by. Elderflower water or elderberry wine are often used in Midsummer rituals. Elder is also used at Samhain (Halloween), with branches hung over doors and windows to ward off the many evil and mischievous creatures afoot on that night.

Hazel

Love never dies a natural death.

— Anaïs Nin

Botanical name: *Corylus*

Native to: Northern hemisphere, especially North America, Europe, and Asia

Also called: Hazelnut; *Corylus maxima* is filbert.

Medicinal properties: Can treat stomach ailments, nausea, flu, and other common cold symptoms. The flowers are the part most often used for tea.

Magical properties: Hazel trees are sacred to the dead (as you will see in the following story), so they can be used as wands in invoking spirits and any magic that has to do with passages into the other realms. They are also protecting trees, meant to keep evil or brutish spirits out of the fairy realm, so they can also be used to protect your home.

The Lore

Though we associate the story with a pumpkin, and rightly so, nowhere in fairy tales does hazel make a more heart-wrenching and underrated appearance than in "Cinderella." The Grimm Brothers' version differs quite a bit from the Perrault version, though the key elements remain the same.

Cinderella's mother had died, and her father remarried a woman who was unkind and had two rude daughters. One day, Cinderella's father asked each of the girls what they might want from market. One requested new gowns; the other, jewels. And Cinderella just said, "Father, break off for me the first branch which knocks against your hat on your way home."

Off he rode to market, where he purchased gowns of the finest silk and necklaces of glimmering gold, and on his way home, "as he was riding through a green thicket, a hazel twig brushed against him and knocked off his hat." This, he broke off and took to Cinderella, who took it to her mother's grave.

> Cinderella thanked him, went to her mother's grave and planted the branch on it, and wept so much that the tears fell down on it and watered it. And it grew, however, and became a handsome tree. Thrice a day Cinderella went and sat beneath it, and wept and prayed, and a little white bird always came on the tree, and if Cinderella expressed a wish, the bird threw down to her what she had wished for.

This point is significant because it is actually the tree that later gives her a dress to wear to the king's festival (which takes place over several days). After completing a series of horrendous tasks, including sorting tiny lentil beans from ash—which the birds aid her with—Cinderella was told she still cannot go to the ball because she's got nothing suitable to wear. Off her stepsisters went without her. In the Disney movie version, the birds and mice help make Cinderella's first gown (which the wicked stepsisters later tear to shreds). But in the Grimm version:

> As no one was now at home, Cinderella went to her mother's grave beneath the hazel-tree, and cried,

> "Shiver and quiver, little tree,

> Silver and gold throw down over me."

> Then the bird threw a gold and silver dress down to her, and slippers embroidered with silk and silver. She put on the dress with all speed, and went to the festival.

Delightedly, no one recognized her, and she became the belle of the ball. The prince would dance only with her, but he didn't get her name. He decided to wait and see who she left with, but she escaped early and hid in the pigeon shed. The prince and his father, the king, decided to hack the little shed to pieces, but by the time they got an axe, Cinderella had escaped and run home. She put her old dirty clothes back on, and she took the beautiful gown and shoes and laid them back on her mother's grave beneath the hazel tree, where the little bird took them away and hid them.

The next day the festival began anew, and the stepsisters and Cinderella's parents left to attend. Cinderella waited until they were well gone; then she dashed out to the hazel tree and said:

"Shiver and quiver, my little tree,

Silver and gold throw down over me."

The bird tossed down an even more beautiful gown, much more exquisite than the one before, and she slipped it on and off to the festival she went. Again, her own family didn't recognize her, and the prince had eyes only for her.

When evening arrived, she wished to leave, and the king's son followed her and wanted to see which house she went into. Before he could catch her, she dashed away into the garden and hid in a giant pear tree. The prince waited until Cinderella's father came home, when he explained that he had followed the beautiful woman home to learn her identity, but she escaped into this tree. Her father cut down the tree, but she was not there, for she had jumped down the other side, given the little bird in the hazel tree her dress to hide, and put herself among the kitchen ashes in her old gray gown.

On the third day of the festival, once the coast was clear, Cinderella again went to her mother's grave and said to the hazel tree:

"Shiver and quiver, my little tree,

Silver and gold throw down over me."

And now the bird threw down to her a dress which was more splendid and magnificent than any she had yet had, and the slippers were golden.

Again, the king's son would only dance with her. Again, she escaped from him, but this time he had put pitch (tar) all over the staircase, and one of her slippers stuck in it. She escaped anyway, but now he at least had a way to identify her. He declared he would only marry the woman whose foot was made for this golden slipper.

If you think you know what happens next, you may be surprised. The king's son did indeed bring the slipper around, straight to Cinderella's house, where he had seen her run into the garden. One of the stepsisters immediately sat down and tried to shove the slipper on her foot, but she couldn't get one toe in.

Then her mother gave her a knife and said, "Cut the toe off; when thou art Queen thou wilt have no more need to go on foot." The maiden cut the toe off, forced the foot into the shoe, swallowed the pain, and went out to the King's son. Then he took her on his horse as his bride and rode away with her. They were, however, obliged to pass the grave, and there, on the hazel-tree, sat the two pigeons and cried,

"Turn and peep, turn and peep,

There's blood within the shoe,

The shoe it is too small for her,

The true bride waits for you."

At this, the prince looked down and saw the blood filling up the shoe. He turned around and brought her home. The other sister seized her chance and tried to put the bloody shoe on her own foot. She could get all of her toes in but not her heel.

So, her mother gave her a knife and said, "Cut a bit off thy heel; when thou art Queen thou wilt have no more need to go on foot." The maiden cut a bit off her heel, forced her foot into the shoe, swallowed the pain, and went out to the King's son. He took her on his horse as his bride, and rode away with her, but when they passed by the hazel-tree, two little pigeons sat on it and cried,

"Turn and peep, turn and peep,

There's blood within the shoe,

The shoe it is too small for her,

The true bride waits for you."

Again, he looked down and saw the blood gushing from the shoe. The king's son turned around and brought her back home. But the prince *knew* this was the house he had seen the mysterious maiden run to. He asked Cinderella's father if there were any other daughters, and the father replied that there was just Cinderella, who was in the kitchen, covered in ash and did not attend the ball. The prince insisted on seeing her, so Cinderella washed her hands and face, and walked into the room where the prince was holding the golden shoe. She sat down on a little stool and slid her foot into the slipper, which, of course, fit perfectly.

And when she rose up and the King's son looked at her face he recognized the beautiful maiden who had danced with him and cried, "That is the true bride!" The stepmother and the two sisters were terrified and became pale with rage; he, however, took Cinderella on his horse and rode away with her. As they passed by the hazel-tree, the two white doves cried—

"Turn and peep, turn and peep,

No blood is in the shoe,

The shoe is not too small for her,

The true bride rides with you."

And if you think you know what happens next, you mostly do. Except that right before the happily ever after, the evil stepsisters attended the wedding, and just before they entered the church, pigeons pecked out their eyes. Grimm enough for you?

Ivy

*He staggered on under the weight of the corpse until
he reached Kiltown Abbey, a ruin festooned with ivy,
where the brown owl hooted all night long, and the
forgotten dead slept around the walls under dense,
matted tangles of brambles and ben-weed.*

—William Butler Yeats, *Fairy and Folk Tales of Ireland*

Botanical name: *Hedera helix*

Native to: Europe, western Asia, British Isles, and northern Africa

Also called: English ivy

Medicinal properties: As a houseplant, ivy is thought to help purify the air. Topically, it can help treat burns. Both folk medicine and modern studies have shown ivy can be used to treat upper respiratory infections.

Magical properties: Everlasting love, immortality, friendship, luck, prosperity. Ivy is difficult to kill and thrives even in winter, so magically, it is used to represent something binding and enduring. A branch of ivy was once a traditional wedding gift. Because it is a tenacious plant, it represents prosperity, success, good luck, happiness, enduring friendship, and money and can be used for any and all of these magical endeavors.

The Lore

When my mother was a little girl in San Francisco, she used to climb the hills behind her house, up, up, up the winding paths of San Bruno Mountain. Today, these ridges are developed and multi-million-dollar houses perch there, taking in the breathtaking expanse of the San Francisco Bay. But back then, there were secret pathways that zigzagged all over the dry grass of the mountain. One of these paths led to an old mansion. My mother used to sneak onto the grounds and sit in the backyard beside a swimming pool that was overgrown with ivy. The house was not itself abandoned. It was occupied, presumably by a shut-in with considerable wealth who no longer had need for the once-glamorous backyard. Where pool parties once splashed, ivy crept, shifting the brick and cracking the travertine. My mother told me this story many times, long after the houses were built on the hill, and I would imagine what it was like to escape into the San Bruno mountains with the butterflies and wild fennel, and what it was like to peer through the gate at an enchanted garden, where ivy reigned supreme.

Take away the ivy, and the enchantment looks more like neglect, the bottom of the pool cracked and dirty. What appears as fairy tale becomes fodder for a horror story. The ivy lends a natural magic to the story, breathing life into an otherwise empty space in the mansion's backyard.

Ivy is one of the few plants you'll find verdant in the heart of winter. Along with holly, it is one of the plants that has been associated with the winter holidays for centuries. Wreaths and garlands of ivy were strewn about the house to bring a festive air when most of the other plants were brown and dormant. This may well be why ivy has earned its association as a plant of immortality, as well as a sacred plant for graveyards. It is thought to be sacred to the dead, and its appearance on headstones represents the concept of life everlasting.

In Ireland, ivy is also associated with Samhain, or All Hallows' Eve, when the dead are honored and wreaths of ivy (again, abundantly green in late October) are placed upon graves and monuments.

W. B. Yeats describes a fairy doctor, a person who works with the fairies for knowledge but is not considered a witch (by his definition, witches work with malignant sprits and fairy doctors with the good, though sometimes mischievous, fairy folk):

> *The most celebrated fairy doctors are sometimes people the fairies loved and carried away, and kept with them for seven years; not that those the fairies' love are always carried off—they may merely grow silent and strange, and take to lonely wanderings in the "gentle" places.*

Yeats then provides a description that he attributes to Lady Wilde, who tells a tale of a man who was a fairy doctor:

> *Winter and summer his dress is the same—merely a flannel shirt and coat. He will pay his share at a feast, but neither eats nor drinks of the food and drink set before him. He speaks no English, and never could be made to learn the English tongue, though he says it might be used with great effect to curse one's enemy. He holds a burial-ground sacred and would not carry away so much as a leaf of ivy from a grave.*

In his book *Ireland's Wild Plants: Myths, Legends, and Folklore*, author Niall Mac Coitir describes ivy's use in love divination, citing a traditional, and delightfully creepy, Irish rhyme involving the use of nine ivy leaves:

> *Nine ivy leaves I place under my head*
>
> *To dream of the living and not of the dead*
>
> *To dream of the man I am going to wed*
>
> *And to see him tonight at the foot of my bed.*

Niall also describes a traditional love ritual used in Wales at Halloween time in which a pointed ivy leaf representing a male and a rounded leaf representing a female are placed together into a fire. If the leaves move toward one another, the couple is destined for love. Away, the relationship is doomed. Easily adaptable for two men or two women—just choose the appropriately shaped leaves. And in another means of divination, in Scotland, it was said young women would put a sprig of ivy at their bosom and the first man thereafter who would speak to them would be their soulmate.

In his seminal collection *British Goblins: Welsh Folk-Lore, Fairy Mythology, Legends, and Traditions*, William Wirt Sikes explores the various colors of fairy dress. Sikes, incidentally, was a writer and journalist appointed to the US Consulate in Wales in 1876. During his time in Wales, he made it his mission to document as many of the old ways and stories that he encountered, not unlike W. B. Yeats did in Ireland. Sikes writes:

> It will be observed that one of the points in this curious speculation rests on the green dress of the fairies. I do not call attention to it with any Quixotic purpose of disputing the conclusion it assists; it is far more interesting as one feature of the general subject of fairies' attire. The Welsh fairies are described with details as to colour in costume not commonly met with in fairy tales, a fact to which I have before alluded. In the legend of the Place of Strife, the Tylwyth Teg encountered by the women are called 'the old elves of the blue petticoat.' A connection with the blue of the sky has here been suggested. It has also been pointed out that the sacred Druidical dress was blue. The blue petticoat fancy seems to be local to North Wales. In Cardiganshire, the tradition respecting an encampment called Moyddin, which the fairies frequented, is that they were always in green dresses, and were never seen there but in the vernal month of May. There is a Glamorganshire goblin called the Green Lady of Caerphilly, the colour of whose dress is indicated by her title. She haunts the ruin of Caerphilly Castle at night, wearing a green robe, and has the power of turning herself into ivy and mingling with the ivy growing on the wall.

According to Joseph Meyer, the leaves of the English ivy are considered a stimulant and contain insecticidal properties. The berries are emetic and cathartic. The ancient Greeks thought ivy would prevent intoxication. And Lesley Bremness, in her *Complete Book of Herbs*, describes the cosmetic use of ivy to relieve sunburn and other toxins in the skin. Some herbalists even insist that ivy can be used to treat cellulite.

Similar to cabbage, ivy was believed to be an antidote to becoming overly intoxicated with wine or ale and as such was once used as a symbol for Bacchus. Crowns of ivy were placed upon the heads of those who were entering into Bacchanalia, to keep them from getting too drunk, it seems. Purveyors of wine and spirits would use an ivy symbol above their door or tavern sign and would set out a green ivy plant to indicate they had the good stuff. It was also once thought that a crown of ivy would give you the ability to spot a witch.

Juniper

We'll just lay here, by the juniper/
While the moon is bright.

—from Joan Baez's rendition of the folk song "Copper Kettle"

Botanical name: *Juniperus* sp.

Native to: Europe, Asia, and North America

Also called: Mountain yew

Of note: As Amy Stewart writes in her delightful cocktail-meets-botany book, *The Drunken Botanist*, junipers are members of the ancient cypress family, which were around 250 million years ago, which means they existed on Pangea. Before there were continents, there was juniper, and therefore, the exact same species, not just cultivars, can be native to entirely different continents.

Medicinal properties: Juniper (especially juniper berries) is one of the oldest medicines around. The berries contain several vital components, including α-Pinene, myrcene, and limonene. The berries relieve stomach pain and nausea and give a beautiful flavoring to gin. The Dine' (Navajo) use a preparation of tea made from juniper berries to help restore a woman's strength after childbirth.

Magical properties: Juniper can be used to ward off sickness and in spells for health, healing, and even resurrection. It has a direct connection with the dead and can be used in spirit communication.

The Lore

While I can't deny that I love a good gin and tonic, it is the principal plant behind the flavor of gin that I love even more. As a teenager, I remember us witchy girls eating the berries to stave off menstrual pains (they're a little harsh when raw, might I add). And while juniper has a host of delightful medicinal qualities, its magic may be more intriguing.

Juniper's association with the dead goes back to ancient times. The Greeks consecrated juniper to the Furies and burned it in their honor, hoping to appease them. Juniper berries were also burned during funerals to keep malignant forces at bay. The strong odor is beloved by many, and witches love it for spells of protection and love. An Italian tradition of hanging up juniper during the winter holidays stems from the story that the Virgin Mary was fleeing with infant Jesus and took shelter from the soldiers of King Herod among its branches. Juniper wood is often burned to bring good luck and break hexes. Juniper may be brushed over doorways and windowsills and placed near baby's cribs to protect and ward off sickness.

It's the following story that gave me the idea for this book to begin with. Like certain fairy tales that you hear as a child, this one stuck with me. It's haunting, and full of gruesome acts, but at the center of it all is a tree—a botanical hero if ever there was one. I have taken the liberty of retelling it here in my own way.

Once upon a time there was a man, and he was a good man, though misfortune seemed to find him. He and his wife wished for a child, and one day she was in the courtyard standing near a fragrant juniper tree, paring an apple, when she cut her finger. Her blood fell upon the snow, and the woman sighed and said, "If only I had a child that was as red as blood and pale as the snow." In a month's time she found she was pregnant, and she made a tea of the juniper berries to keep her nausea at bay. This tree was of great comfort and healing to her throughout her pregnancy, and one day she said to her husband, "If I die, bury me beneath this tree." And in eight months more she gave birth to a beautiful son who was as pale as the snow with ruby red lips. The woman gazed upon her child, but then something was suddenly wrong, and before another moment had passed, the woman died. The man buried her with much sorrow beneath the juniper tree.

Time passed and the man remarried, and he and his new wife had a daughter. The stepmother was terribly jealous of the son, but the boy and his sister adored one another. One day the girl asked her mother for an apple. The mother kept the apples locked away in a big iron chest because apples were a rarity in that part of the world, and also the cold iron kept them fresh. The mother obliged, but then the girl asked for another for her brother. Just then the boy was coming up the lane on his way home from school, and a terrible thought seized the stepmother, and she threw an apple into a great iron chest. When the boy got inside the house, he saw his sister with an apple, and she declared that mother had one for him too! Hungry, he went to his stepmother and politely asked for an apple. The stepmother told him to grab one for himself, and she unlocked the chest, but as he reached in to get one, she slammed the lid down and chopped off his head, which tumbled in among the shiny red apples.

Realizing what she had done and terrified she would be caught, she propped up the boy, tied on his head with a little handkerchief, and put an apple in his hand. The little sister came along and asked the boy for an apple, but he ignored her. So the mother said, "Just give him a little shove!" and when she did, the brother's head fell right off. Quickly, the mother said, "Oh! What have you done to your brother?" The little girl was hysterical, and the mother said, "We must hide this, so that you are not caught." And wickedly, she cut him into pieces, and to disguise it all, she cooked him and made him into black puddings, salted by the tears of his sister, who could not stop crying.

When the father came home, the stepmother made up a story that the boy had asked to visit with his uncle for several weeks, and the father, though surprised, seemed to accept this excuse. Then he sat to dinner and ate up the black pudding, throwing the bones beneath the table. The sister didn't eat a thing but waited, and when her parents had left the kitchen, she gathered all of her dead brother's bones in a silk handkerchief and took them out to bury them next to his mother beneath the juniper tree. At this, the tree began to shift and stir, and a mist swirled about, and suddenly she felt as if her brother were with her again. A little bird was in the tree and saw all of this. He flew away and landed on the windowsill of a nearby cobbler's shop. And it sang:

> My mother she killed me
>
> My father he ate me
>
> My sister she cries in sorrow
>
> As I lie below
>
> Stick, stock, stone dead.

The cobbler was enchanted by the little bird and the pretty song, but he was not sure he'd heard it quite right. To the bird, he said, "Sing me again that beautiful song."

The bird replied, "I will sing for you if you give me those pretty red shoes you're making."

And the cobbler gave the bird the shoes, and the bird sang the eerie song again.

Next the bird flew to the windowsill of the watchmaker's shop. And the bird sang:

> My mother she killed me,
>
> My father he ate me,
>
> My sister she cries in sorrow,
>
> As I lie below.
>
> Stick, stock, stone dead.

"Such a beautiful song!" cried the watchmaker, "But I did not hear the words the first time. Sing it again, little bird!"

"I will sing it for you if you give me that gold watch and chain," said the bird.

And the watchmaker obliged, and the bird sang the song again. Then the bird flew away, holding the red shoes with one claw and the beautiful golden watch and chain in the other. The bird flew to the mill, where three millers were chiseling a large millstone. The bird perched in a tree nearby and sweetly sang:

My mother she killed me,

My father he ate me,

My sister she cries in sorrow,

As I lie below.

Stick!

And at this one of the men put down his tools and looked up at the bird.

Stock!

Then the second miller's man stopped working and looked up.

Stone!

And the third miller's man set aside his tools and looked up.

Dead!

At this, all three men cried in unison, "Oh precious bird, please sing that song to us again!"

To which the bird replied: "I will sing it again if you will put that millstone round my neck."

The men obliged, and the bird sang the song one more time before flying away. The bird flew back toward its home, and landed on the roof where it could see the juniper tree from its perch. Then it dragged the millstone against the tin of the roof.

The wicked stepmother said, "Oh, how it thunders!"

The little girl ran out to see if she could see lightning in the sky, and as she ran, the bird dropped the little red shoes at her feet. Again, the bird rattled the millstone against the roof, and again the stepmother said, "It thunders!" This time the father ran out of the house, and the bird dropped the gold watch and chain.

The little chain caught around the father's wrist, and he caught the watch in his hand. Delighted, he cried out, "Ah! What wonderful gifts the thunder brings us!" The stepmother looked out the window and saw the girl with the shiny red shoes and her husband with a gold watch. The bird dragged the millstone again across the tin roof.

"What gifts will the thunder leave for me?" she wondered as she ran out of the door. Just as she did, the bird dropped the millstone on her head, killing her.

Hearing the commotion, the father and his daughter ran out, and saw the wife dead on the ground, and a great deal of smoke and fire rising up around the juniper tree. And there, also, was her brother, and they were together again at last.

Juniper would appear to be potent in dreams; thus, it is unlucky to dream of the tree itself, especially if the person be sick; but to dream of gathering the berries, if it be in winter, denotes prosperity; whilst to dream of the actual berries signifies that the dreamer will shortly arrive at great honours, and become an important person.
—Richard Folkard, *Plant Lore, Legends, and Lyrics*

Oak

Hoarsely to the midnight moon
Voiced the oak his rugged rune:
"Harken, sibyl Moon, to me;
Hear the saga of the Tree."

—William Henry Venable

Botanical name: *Quercus* spp.

Native to: Northern hemisphere: North America, Central America, Asia, Europe, Ireland, UK

Also called: King of the forest, *dair*

Medicinal properties: Leaves and barks can treat wounds, sores, bug bites, bleeding, and other skin conditions. Oak has been used as cough medicine and is good for sore throat and general colds. It is antidiarrheal, anti-inflammatory, and antiseptic.

Magical properties: Oaks represent wisdom and leadership. Use oak leaves when you wish to contact the protecting spirits of the oaks, including fairies and seek knowledge from them. Oak leaves can help students concentrate. Acorns are a symbol of abundance, fertility, and renewal.

The Lore

Across the main road and down a path stood the great oak. Though it was technically not on our property, my mother would often take my sister, brother, and me on walks to this tree. In it was a small hollow, not unlike that we heard of in the story of the birch tree. No robber's cache was hidden here, but my mom and a couple of the neighborhood women would meet occasionally to go for walks at night and leave treasures in the nook in this oak tree. They wouldn't say much about when or where they'd meet, but it was always in the full moonlight. We were encouraged to visit the oak (during the day) and admire its smooth bark and its heavy limbs that looked as if they could support the weight of the world. We'd gather the small acorns it dropped. In a forest of skinny pines, the mighty oak stood out. It had withstood at least a hundred years of life in the foothills.

What we were doing was an age-old tradition that would make the Druids proud. Oak trees have long been the center of stories and myths, a great keeper of the mysteries, and not quick to give up those secrets. Oak trees were sacred to Druids, who held ceremonies and important council beneath them, and sacred rites were performed with their leaves. The Druids also used the bark and leaves of oak as medicine. Pliny the Elder said that oak and mistletoe were the most sacred of all the trees to the Druids. Fairy folk are fond of the oak, dancing beneath its canopy and holding their own sacred rites and revelry there. In ancient Rome, *Querquetulanae virae* are the dryads, the feminine tree spirits of the oak grove. It is from them that we have the Latin name for oak, *Quercus*. These dryads were reclusive but loved the goddess Artemis. In many cultures the oak was equated with leadership, heroism, and wisdom, so wreaths of oak were donned by kings, gods, and soldiers alike and were worn in ceremony, battle, and victory parades.

In North America, oaks are abundant and so were (and are) widely utilized by native cultures. The acorns can be ground into a meal to make bread, cakes, or

mush and pressed for oil. Acorns (and oaks) contain a high amount of tannins, which have medicinal qualities but also make things taste bitter. These tannins were leached out before use in the case of all species except for one, *Quercus lobata*, the white oak. The Miwok, Pomo, and Yuk especially prize this oak for its large acorns that were sweeter and could be eaten without leaching. The leaves and bark especially were used to treat a variety of ailments, both topical and internal, ranging from dysentery to bug bites.

In *The Fairy-Faith in Celtic Countries*, W. Y. Evans-Wentz recorded this charm from a woman in Cornwall:

> My old nurse, Betty Grancan, used to say that you could call up the troll at the Tolcarne if while there you held in your hand three dried leaves, one of the ash, one of the oak, and one of the thorn, and pronounced an incantation or charm. Betty would never tell me the words of the charm, because she said I was too much of a sceptic. The words of such a Cornish charm had to pass from one believer to another, through a woman to a man, and from a man to a woman, and thus alternately.

It is difficult to separate oak lore from that of the sacred mistletoe. Mistletoe is the common name of several plants that fall within the order *Santales*. Though sometimes mislabeled as a parasitic plant, mistletoe in fact is a hemiparasite, a plant that gains nourishment from the host plant but one that is able to photosynthesize, so the relationship is more symbiotic than parasitic. The more familiar plants we know as mistletoe include the most common European variety, *Viscum album,* and the North American species, *Phoradendron serotinum*, both of which are widely harvested during winter months. In Celtic lore, the mistletoe was sacred because while all the leaves were gone in winter, it showed signs of life. Druids would only harvest mistletoe with a golden sickle. Some believe mistletoe to be the Golden Bough of myth, which opened the world of the dead.

In Norse mythology, we have the story of Balder, who had prophesized his own death. To protect him, his mother, Frigg, went to all of the things upon the Earth, the plants, the stones, the metals, the water, and the animals and made them swear never to hurt him. She didn't bother with the mistletoe, which was just a little sprig (it was probably in the fall when not much was made of the plant yet). The trickster Loki got the blind god Höðr to shoot an arrow poisoned with mistletoe at Balder, and he died. The gods made mistletoe promise only to do things for love and not misfortune, and this may well be why we kiss beneath it to this day.

Mistletoe, specifically *Viscum*, is full of powerful medicine. Certain species of *Viscum* have been studied for their anticancer properties, so maybe mistletoe really is trying to make amends.

What were known as oak apples are oak galls, formed when wasps lay their eggs in oak leaves. They were once widely used as a source of ink.

Pine

Faint murmurs from the pine-tops reach my ear,
As if a harp-string—touched in some far sphere—
Vibrating in the lucid atmosphere,
Let the soft south wind waft its music here.

—Thomas Bailey Aldrich, "Among the Pines"

Botanical name: *Pinus* spp.

Native to: Primarily northern hemisphere but some species are found in the southern hemisphere

Also called: Sometimes pinyon

Medicinal properties: Pine trees treat tooth pain, coughs, colds, and even thyroid diseases. Pine and pine resin have antiseptic qualities and can be used to treat fevers, tuberculosis, urinary tract infections, and externally for wounds, burns, and lacerations.

Magical properties: Pine represents longevity, immortality, and unflappability, so use pine when you wish to overcome obstacles and stay the course.

The Lore

It was on a bed of pine needles that I first learned the language of the forest. We'd moved far into the countryside, leaving the heady brugmansia and ladened lemon tree of the Bay Area for the pine-scattered hills of California's Gold Country. With little else on my agenda—I had no friends yet, school hadn't started, and we didn't have a television or even electricity—I spent hours playing in the forest, making a fort with a soft bed of pine needles, inhaling the scent of summer in the foothills. That distinct, acrid scent of pine needles on a warm day will always smell like home to me. I experimented in many ways with the pine trees, which were new plants to me. I picked the needles, braided them, nibbled on them, and used them as miniature swords against my sister.

There are more than one hundred species of pine around the world, with all but one native to the northern hemisphere. They scrabble on hillsides in Italy and bow gracefully in the snow of Finnish forests. In California alone there are twenty-nine native species, from low-growing coastal trees to towering sugar pines that drop pine cones over a foot long. In every culture where pine trees grow, they are revered for their practical properties: they make excellent boards, provide disease-resistant wood, and produce pine cones, which can be used for fuel. Pine nuts are eaten as food. Pine trees produce medicine in the form of the bark, needles, resin, and fruits (pine cones and pine nuts) that can be used to treat everything from common colds to tooth pain to tuberculosis.

The pine was dedicated to Bacchus/Dionysus, and its branches were often used to decorate during the Dionysian festivals. Pine resin or pine-infused wine is still a thing today, where Greek wine is often flavored with pine cones.

Pitys is the dryad who lived in a pine tree. As a beautiful young woman, she was pursued relentlessly by more than one god, including Boreas, the god of the cold north wind. There are versions of this story that say she was changed by Pan because he loved her, or because he was trying to hide her, or both. Others say she was chased off a cliff by Boreas, and it was Gaia who took pity on her and transformed her lifeless body into a pine tree.

An old Roman legend tells of two lovers who were buried side by side. One was changed into a pine tree, the other into a vine, that they might always embrace. This is similar to the rose and the briar, where out of one grave comes a single rose and the other the thorny briar. The rose, of course, grows around the briar. Pines and pine cones are symbols of immortality, and when seen on a headstone or in a decorative concrete funerary urn in a cemetery, they mean that the person will forever be immortalized and that the person was incorruptible. Pine is an enduring wood and its resin also lasts, so it represents resiliency and trustworthiness. Boughs of pine and fir were used to cover coffins, and pine is one of the primary woods traditionally used to make coffins.

There is one story that involves pine that we likely all know by heart, and that is the story of Pinocchio, the little boy carved from wood. Although in the story the little log that will become Pinocchio is described as being "just a log" or a simple piece of nondescript wood, *Pino* literally translates to pine tree in Italian. The term *pinnochia* or *pinonchio* translates to pine nut in the Tuscan dialect. We can make a pretty easy inference that Pinocchio is made of pine. Published by Carlo Collodi in 1883, *The Adventures of Pinocchio* was immediately one of the most popular children's books in Italy. Carol Della Chiesa's translation from the original Italian was published a few decades later. It reads:

> Once upon a time there was a piece of wood. It was not an expensive piece of wood. Far from it. Just a common block of firewood, one of those thick, solid logs that are put on the fire in winter to make cold rooms cozy and warm.

As the Maestro Cherry (so named for the tip of his nose being red, an attribute we see in Disney's Geppetto) is about to carve the chunk of wood into a table leg, he hears a voice saying "Ouch!" and "Don't hit me so hard!" This gives the man quite a fright, but he rather quickly accepts that the wood is enchanted, so he gives it to his friend Geppetto, who carves it into a marionette. In the original story, Pinocchio is much more of a rabble-rouser, and well before he's carved, too, causing Geppetto to come to blows with his friend, Maestro Cherry. Pinocchio stirs up all kinds of trouble, and once he's carved into a marionette, becomes a bit of a nightmare. He strikes out on his own and one night "falls asleep with his feet on a foot warmer, and awakens the next day with his feet all burned off." Also, in this version:

- Pinocchio kills the Talking Cricket with a hammer.

- The Blue Fairy isn't called that, and she's not a fairy; she's a ghost (at least at first).

- The Lovely Maiden with the Azure Hair first appears in a cottage in the woods, where she tells Pinocchio she is dead and just looking out the window, waiting for her coffin.

- He encounters robbers-assassins who want to take his money, which they learn he has while they are all dining at "The Inn of the Red Lobster" (I am *not* making this up!).

- The assassins try to hang Pinocchio from a tree in the forest, where he dangles for three hours with his eyes open and his legs kicking.

- The Lovely Maiden with the Azure Hair, who keeps on looking out the window waiting for her coffin, sees him dangling and sends a falcon to get Pinocchio down, which in turn reveals her true identity as a fairy.

- Three "doctors" attend Pinocchio, one of whom is the Talking Cricket (whaa??). The other two are a crow and an owl.

- He's nursed back to health on sugar water and then lies to the fairy about having gold. His nose grows.

- The Blue Fairy dies. But not really.

Eventually, Pinocchio reunites with the Blue Fairy, who isn't actually dead (again) and promises to turn him into a real boy so that he isn't living a life of danger (most recently he was captured by a farmer who tried to make him his watchdog and a fisherman who tried to fry him in a pan). But he runs off and joins the circus, gets turned into a donkey, and becomes the star of the show. When he doesn't perform up to standards, he's tossed into the sea, where he is swallowed by a shark (not a whale). On the plus side, once he hits the water, he shapeshifts back into a marionette. Inside the shark, he meets up with Geppetto, who was swallowed up in his little boat trying to rescue Pinocchio. They almost drown swimming back to shore, but in the end they make it, and Pinocchio vows to be a kinder, better person. For that, he is rewarded by being transformed into real boy. Geppetto is turned into a younger, more talented, wealthier man, and they all live happily ever after. Quite the adventure for a little pine log.

Pine branches are lit at Nordic Midsummer festivals to light the way for Balder's descent into darkness.

CHAPTER 6

The Marsh King's Daughter

Plants That Grow Near Streams, Bogs, Lakes, and the Sea

SEAWEED • WATER LILY • WILLOW

The Girl Who Trod on a Loaf

There was once a wretched little girl who had been sent to live in a very wealthy family's foster house, where she had promptly been spoiled rotten. When the girl was sent to visit her poor parents and bring them "a loaf of good wheaten bread," she moaned and groaned a bit but eventually put on her finest outfit and her fanciest shoes and set out. When she came to a section of the path near the marsh, she discovered it quite mucky and, instead of soiling her precious shoes, she threw down the loaf of bread to step on it to get across the puddle. As soon as she alighted upon the bread, it—and she—began to sink slowly into the brackish mire and into the hall of the Marsh-wife. There she remained for years, in a state of suspended animation, like a statue.

> When she came to a place where the path went over marshy ground, and there was water and mud over a long piece of the way, she threw the bread down into the mud to step on it and get across dryshod. But as she stood with one foot on the loaf and lifted the other, the loaf sank down with her deeper and deeper, and she disappeared wholly, and nothing was to be seen but a black bubbling pool.
>
> That's the story.

Where did she go to? Why, she went down to the Marshwoman who brews. The Marshwoman is aunt to the Elf girls—they are well enough known, there are ballads about them and they have had their pictures taken—but about the Marshwoman people only know that when the meadows steam in summer time it is because the Marshwoman is brewing. It was down into her brewery that Inger sank, and that's not a place you can stand for long. The dustbin is a brilliant drawing-room compared with the Marshwoman's brewery. Every vat stinks enough to make you faint away, and the vats stand thick together, and if there is anywhere a tiny opening between them where you could squeeze through, you can't, because of all the damp toads and fat snakes that cluster together there. Down there sank little Inger. All that horrible live mess was so icy cold that she shuddered through all her limbs and stiffened with it more and more. The loaf stuck fast to her and drew her as an amber button draws a bit of straw.

My mother read me Hans Christian Andersen's "The Girl Who Trod on the Loaf"—which the above story is excerpted from—when I was about the age of Inger, the little girl in the story. She read it to my sister and me by the light of kerosene lamp. We were living in a little trailer by a river, and during the day, the parking lot filled with swimmers and trail hikers, but at night, it was a different place entirely. The parking lot was empty, except for a few other intrepid campers on the weekends. The river continued rushing, as it will, but without the chatter of children playing and scratchy music coming from a sand-worn boombox, the river seemed louder. It seemed hungrier.

This story has always haunted me (spoiler alert, in the Andersen version, the sincere tears of a sweet child, pure of heart, free Inger from the Marsh Queen's brewery).

Recently, while traveling in Ireland, I visited a museum in Dublin with the famous "bog bodies"—including the extraordinarily well-preserved Iron Age corpse of Old Croghan Man. The bodies, perhaps like young Ingrid's was, are believed to be so well intact due to the high acidity and low oxygen of peat bogs.

Bogs, in general, have a dense matting of vegetation and are made up of moss. So dense, in fact, that it can be difficult to discern what is dry land and what gives way to a slick, slovenly mess. For a young child or an errant sheep, this could prove fatal. So naturally, steering clear of soggy bottoms is a great survival tactic.

I still have the same copy of the book that my mother read to me. On a different page there is the story of the Marsh King's Daughter, describing a great mossy bog that you can also sink into if you don't know where to step. It's a beautiful passage, describing everything rather pleasantly:

> The moss lies where was once the bottom of the sea, before the great upheaval of the land; and now it stretches for miles, surrounded on all sides by watery meadows and quivering bog, with turf-moss cloudberries and stunted trees growing. A fog hangs over it almost continually, and till about seventy years ago wolves were still found there. It may certainly be called a wild moor, and you can imagine what lack of paths and what abundance of swamp and sea was there thousands of years ago. In that waste man saw ages back just what he sees to-day. The reeds were just as high, with the same kind of long leaves and purplish-brown, feathery flowers as they have now; the birches stood with white bark and fine, loose-hung leaves just as they now stand.

Sounds pretty idyllic, right? Until...

> Whoever it was, poor peasant or free hunter, that trod on the quagmire, it happened thousands of years ago just as it does to-day—in he went and down he sank, down to the Marsh King, as they called him, who reigned beneath in the great Moss Kingdom. He was called also the Mire King, but we will call him by the stork's name for him—Marsh King. People know very little about how he governed, but perhaps that is just as well.

Marshes, mosses, boggy glens. Wild rivers that spill into cool lochs. Stagnant lakes and bubbling brooks. And the thrashing sea. So although we often think of the dirt of a garden bed and forest floor to keep our plants alive, there are those that prefer the life aquatic. From water lilies to water horses, won't you join me for a little swim?

 Seaweed

A mermaid found a swimming lad,
Picked him for her own,
Pressed her body to his body,
Laughed; and plunging down
Forgot in cruel happiness
That even lovers drown.

—William Butler Yeats

Botanical name: *Nereocystis luetkeana* (bull kelp); *Porpyhra* sp. (kelp); *Postelsia palmaeformis* (sea palm); *Uva lactuca Linnacus* (sea lettuce). *Alaria esculenta* (murlins); *Palmaria palmata* (red algae, dulse); *Saccharina latissimi* (Irish kelp, sweet kelp); *Chondrus crispus* (Carrageen or Irish moss)

Native to: The ocean as well as other bodies of water

Also called: See preceding names.

Of note: *Seaweed* is a common term used to describe thousands of species of marine algae. For the purpose of this book, I've identified a few key species most commonly used in food and medicine.

Medicinal properties: Seaside communities have harvested seaweed for thousands of years as a source of food and medicine. Many types of seaweed have anti-inflammatory properties and can be used to treat swelling, cuts, and burns. Some seaweeds have anticancer properties that are being studied for use in cancer treatment drugs. Seaweed has essential nutrients, including iron and fiber. Some seaweed species can be high in protein. Seaweed such as carrageenan is widely used as a thickening agent in cooking as well as in cosmetics.

Magical properties: Seaweed can be used in rituals of self-care, self-love, and beauty, to provide nourishment to your mind, body, and soul. It can also be used to connect with the mysteries of the ocean and other bodies of water, the secret witchcraft of mermaids, and all of the other aquatic sprits. Seaweed can also help keep you afloat metaphorically during trying times, so can be used in spells for success.

The Lore

At this stage in my life, I feel as though no book I've written is complete unless I at least make mention of mermaids, which brings us to this section on seaweed. Our love affair with these strange aquatic creatures goes back thousands of years ... and probably before that, since before keeping time was a thing. Early records depict an Assyrian goddess, Astargatis, around 1000 BCE as a mermaid. She killed a man she loved and, so ashamed, banned herself to a lake. When that didn't hide her well enough, she became a half-fish, half-woman. The Taino people, the Indigenous people of the Caribbean, speak of Aycayia, a mythical mermaid whose voice has the power to sink ships. Blackbeard feared mermaids so much that he would sail nautical miles out of his way to avoid mermaid-infested waters.

Mermaids possess great skills and healing powers and can grant them in turn. For this reason, mermaids were persecuted during the witch hunts. In John Gregorson's 1900 work, *Superstitions of the Highlands and Islands of Scotland*, he writes about a man who lives in Eilean Anabuich, a small village in the Hebrides who captured a mermaid. She granted him three wishes in exchange for her freedom: he became a prophet who could foretell the future (especially that of women); he gained the ability to sing (which locals say was debatable); and he became a skilled herbal doctor who could cure the King's Evil (tuberculosis) as well as other previously incurable diseases.

The water horse, or kelpie, of Scotland brings seaweed from the sea to inland fields to nourish the crops. But don't be fooled into thinking that's the only thing water horses do. They can easily grab victims and drag them into the water in a flash. Gregorson describes a lonely lake northeast of Mull where a traveler happened by. Feeding along the loch was a horse. When the traveler approached it, he "observed green-water herbs (*liaranaich*) about its feet and refrained from touching it." Later, he was passed by a stranger who told him that if it was a water horse and if it found him to be unfriendly or wishing ill, it would take him right into the water.

Gregorson also writes:

> In Skye it was said to have a sharp bill (*gob biorach*), or, as others describe it, a narrow brown slippery snout. Accounts are uniform that it had a long flowing tail and mane. In colour it was sometimes grey, sometimes black, and sometimes black with a white spot on its forehead. This variation arose, some say, from the water horse being of any colour like other horses, and others say from its having the power of changing its colour as well as its shape. When it came in the shape of a man, it was detected by its horse-hoofs and by the green water weeds or sand in its hair. It was then very amorous, but the end of those who were unfortunate enough to encounter it was to be taken to the loch and devoured. However much benefit the farmer might at first derive from securing one with the cap or cow-shackle he was ultimately involved by it in ruinous loss.

Seaweed is, of course, both an essential nutrient for the soil in many ocean-side gardens and an important food. The Coast Salish harvest seaweed, which is often eaten boiled by itself or with fish or clams. The Kashaya Pomo of the northern California coast harvest several species of seaweed, including sea lettuce and bull kelp. Sea lettuce is used to treat mastitis. Bull kelp strips are sucked on to soothe sore throats. Seaweed can be boiled, baked, formed into cakes, dried, or eaten raw. Seaweed plays a prominent role in Japanese cuisine, with several types served in salads, or the most popular, Nori, which is used in sushi. There is evidence of seaweed being given over 1,200 years ago as a gift to an imperial court in Japan. Seaweed farming is experiencing a renaissance around the world, especially in places like Scotland, Ireland, and California, with more and more people understanding the importance of cultivating this nourishing, abundant food.

Lady Wilde recounts a story of a man called Shaun Mor who lived on Innis-Sark (or Inis Airc, today known as Inishark), Ireland. He hung out at night with the fairy folk. He carried their goods, and in exchange they gave him all kinds of fairy gifts and taught him their secrets. If they ever tried to cross him, he'd strangle them in the seaweed.

Mermaids might be considered the original seaweed farmers, at least if you ask Hans Christian Andersen. By now, you are probably familiar with basics of his short story "The Little Mermaid": a young mermaid craves adventure, decides to take her chances on land, but has to strike a terrible bargain with the sea witch in order to make it above water. Andersen's original tale has quite a few more ghoulish attributes than the more recent versions, but that doesn't mean it's all doom and gloom. I will leave you here, dear reader, with this little excerpt from the original. It is the most beautiful description of an underwater garden:

> Far out in the ocean, where the water is as blue as the prettiest cornflower and as clear as crystal, it is very, very deep; so deep, indeed, that no cable could sound it, and many church steeples, piled one upon another, would not reach from the ground beneath to the surface of the water above. There dwell the Sea King and his subjects.

We must not imagine that there is nothing at the bottom of the sea but bare yellow sand. No, indeed, for on this sand grow the strangest flowers and plants, the leaves and stems of which are so pliant that the slightest agitation of the water causes them to stir as if they had life. Fishes, both large and small, glide between the branches as birds fly among the trees here upon land.

In the deepest spot of all stands the castle of the Sea King. Its walls are built of coral, and the long Gothic windows are of the clearest amber. The roof is formed of shells that open and close as the water flows over them. Their appearance is very beautiful, for in each lies a glittering pearl which would be fit for the diadem of a queen.

The Sea King had been a widower for many years, and his aged mother kept house for him. She was a very sensible woman, but exceedingly proud of her high birth, and on that account wore twelve oysters on her tail, while others of high rank were only allowed to wear six.

She was, however, deserving of very great praise, especially for her care of the little sea princesses, her six granddaughters. They were beautiful children, but the youngest was the prettiest of them all. Her skin was as clear and delicate as a rose leaf, and her eyes as blue as the deepest sea; but, like all the others, she had no feet and her body ended in a fish's tail. All day long they played in the great halls of the castle or among the living flowers that grew out of the walls. The large amber windows were open, and the fish swam in, just as the swallows fly into our houses when we open the windows; only the fishes swam up to the princesses, ate out of their hands, and allowed themselves to be stroked.

Outside the castle there was a beautiful garden, in which grew bright-red and dark-blue flowers, and blossoms like flames of fire; the fruit glittered like gold, and the leaves and stems waved to and fro continually. The earth itself was the finest sand, but blue as the flame of burning sulphur. Over everything lay a peculiar blue radiance, as if the blue sky were everywhere, above and below, instead of the dark depths of the sea. In calm weather the sun could be seen, looking like a reddish-purple flower with light streaming from the calyx.

Each of the young princesses had a little plot of ground in the garden, where she might dig and plant as she pleased. One arranged her flower bed in the form of a whale; another preferred to make hers like the figure of a little mermaid; while the youngest child made hers round, like the sun, and in it grew flowers as red as his rays at sunset.

She was a strange child, quiet and thoughtful. While her sisters showed delight at the wonderful things which they obtained from the wrecks of vessels, she cared only for her pretty flowers, red like the sun, and a beautiful marble statue. It was *the representation of a handsome boy, carved out of pure white stone, which had fallen to the bottom of the sea from a wreck.*

She planted by the statue a rose-colored weeping willow. It grew rapidly and soon hung its fresh branches over the statue, almost down to the blue sands. The shadows had the color of violet and waved to and fro like the branches, so that it seemed as if the crown of the tree and the root were at play, trying to kiss each other.

Iris might not be the first plant that comes to mind when you think of a swamp, but irises thrive in marshy areas. The flower and the part of your eye with color are both named for Iris, the Greek messenger of the gods who traveled on a rainbow. The flower has strong meaning across many cultures. In decoration, including on graves, irises are a symbol of life. *Fleur de lis*, in fact, translates to "flower of life." As much as it's a flower of life, it has strong associations with death and the Underworld. The Greeks put irises on tombs because Iris helped guide souls of dead women. The three leaves of the flower represent faith, wisdom, and valor.

Water Lily

'Water Lilies' is an extension of my life. Without the water the lilies cannot live, as I am without art.

—Claude Monet

Botanical name: *Nymphaeaceae*

Native to: Temperate and tropical climates around the world

Also called: Water nymphs, lotus, padma

Of note: There are at least sixty different plants that fall in the greater water lily family of *Nymphaeaceae*. The more common water lily is *Nymphaea* sp. The fragrant *N. odorata* is native to North America. Monet's water lilies included varieties of *N. odorata* as well as *N. mexicana*. The Egyptian lotus is *N. lotus*, and the sacred lotus is *Nelumbo nucifera*. Amazonian water lily, always worth a mention, is *Victoria amazonica*.

Medicinal properties: The sacred lotus (*Nelumbo nucifera*) is the most widely consumed and is used in traditional medicine in a variety of ways. It is thought to be anti-anxiety and to lower blood pressure; it has even been studied as a treatment for Alzheimer's. In traditional Chinese medicine, lotus seeds are used in a tonic wine to counteract diarrhea and help heal the spleen.

Magical properties: The water lily, or lotus, can represent fertility, enlightenment, beauty, prosperity, power, wisdom, harmony, and knowledge. The color of the lily can changes its meaning, but it can be used for connecting with divine wisdom and all water spirits. Because the water lily grows in mud but purifies the water and offers blooms like a star, it is said to make the world around it a better place.

The Lore

From the walls of Egyptian tombs to the canvas of Claude Monet, water lilies hold an otherworldly quality. The very name invokes the nymphs, water spirits of Greek mythology. The Greeks also say the water lily was once a young girl who was madly in love with Heracles. She died of jealousy and was transformed into the water lily. The water lily and its single bloom represent learning, wisdom, beauty, and the divine feminine in many cultures. Though it may be associated with fertility, it is not a symbol of virility. In ancient Egypt, the lotus was believed to have anti-aphrodisiacal qualities, owing to the association with Osiris. Osiris's body is often seen adorned with them. Osiris was killed by his brother and chopped into pieces, but Isis collected all his parts—minus one—and revived him enough to ensure he could pass on to Ra. However, if you were after an aphrodisiac, you could always try the blue water lily. Early Egyptian tomb paintings also show these lotus flowers being cultivated in ponds, along with papyrus.

The lotus flower plays heavily in the imagery of Hindu mythology. Sarasvati (Saraswati) is the goddess of knowledge, creativity, art, music, and wisdom and is associated with rivers and small bodies of water. She is often depicted seated on a white lotus blossom. The goddess of power, beauty, prosperity and fortune, Lakshmi, is seen standing or sitting on a pink lotus flower. Ganesha, the elephant-headed god who removes obstacles and brings fortune, is also seen on a pink lotus.

In Buddhism the lotus represents enlightenment. The plant grows in mud and has the ability to purify the water around it while also bringing forth great beauty and nourishment.

> Outside in the brook grew many water-lilies, with broad green
> leaves, which looked as if they were swimming about on the
> water. The leaf farthest away was the largest, and to this the old
> toad swam with Thumbelina in her walnut-shell.
> —Andrew Lang, "Thumbelina," *The Yellow Fairy Book*

The rhizomes of the lotus are eaten fresh, cooked, fried, dried, or pickled. The flowers, seeds, and embryos also can be eaten. In China, Korea, and Vietnam, a tea is made from the roots, flowers, and seeds. In Korea, it is called *yeonhwa-cha*.

The Tupi–Guarani, Indigenous people of Brazil, have a story surrounding the giant water lily (*Victoria amazonica*). Naia, the daughter of the tribal leader, became so enchanted with Jaci, the moon goddess, that she began dreaming of becoming a star herself. Each night she would go out and try to touch the moon. On the night of one full moon, the moon reflected perfectly in the water of a river, and Naia jumped in. She drowned, but Jaci took pity on her and transformed her into a star on earth, the giant water lily's blossom.

Though it was described by botanist Thaddeus Haenke in 1801, the first recorded "discovery" of the giant Amazon water lily was made by Eduard Poeppig, who named it *Euryale amazonica*. Later, Robert Schomburgk "rediscovered" it on expedition and sent back his notes and detailed drawings to John Lindley, botanist for the Crown. While this remarkable species was already well known to the Tupi–Guarani people, when it was brought back to England, it was a marvel to behold. The specimen was housed in a special conservatory built for it at Kew Gardens and nursed along until it bloomed. Lindley presented Queen Victoria with this bloom and told her this rare flower was to be named for her: *Victoria regina*. However, Poeppig had already entered it into the botanical records as *Euryale amazonica*.

The record is a little hazy on who got to it first, but in the end, the taxonomical evidence didn't lie: according to the rules of botany, it was a *Euryale amazonica*. A secret debate ensued, as no one wanted to offend the queen. In one camp, there were the botanists who said it was *Victoria regina* because (1) it had previously been named that and not recorded; (2) they'd already told the queen; and (3), botanically speaking it couldn't be a *Euryale*. In the other camp, there were those who said its name couldn't be changed, and even if it was described as *Victoria regina*, the botanical name had already been made official. Incidentally, *Euryale* is another genus that falls under the *Nymphaeaceae* umbrella and includes the curious prickly water lily, *Euryale ferox*. Euryale was one of the Gorgons, sister to Medusa. After much debate, a compromise was proposed: *Victoria amazonica*. But no one wanted to tell the queen. Some felt her name being associated with the Amazon was undignified: these were horrifically ethnocentric times when the Amazon was considered full of savages and not fit for a queen. Others just didn't want to offend her by taking the name away. So they decided that the name would be kept secret. When she died, they changed the botanical record and labeled it properly. Until 2022, it was believed to be the largest water lily in the world, but that title now belongs to *Victoria boliviana*.

The *Victoria amazonica*, previously considered the largest species of water lily, can grow to up to 8 feet in diameter. It can support about 60 pounds on average, but some pads have been known to support up to 160 pounds.

In Lang's *The Blue Fairy Book*, we find a story called "The Water-Lily, the Gold Spinners." In it, three maidens lived in the forest with an old woman who was a witch. Every day the three girls spun flax into thread, from sunrise to sunset. Every few weeks the woman would disappear for the day, never telling where she'd gone. Before leaving, she would caution the girls to stay inside and not talk to anyone, especially a man, if one should happen by. No one ever came that deep into the forest, so they laughed and kept spinning. The day came for the witch to leave. As was her custom, she told the girls to keep spinning and—under no circumstances—to wander. As it happened, that same day along came a prince, lost in the woods.

The older two kept spinning, but the youngest girl couldn't help but stay in the company of the prince.

Three days went by, and the prince was still sitting with the maiden, who had lost all track of time and whose golden thread had lost all of its shine. His cavalry found him, but not before he asked the maiden for her hand in marriage, promising to return. Meanwhile the witch came back that night, saw the dull thread, and knew what was up. She forbid the girl from seeing him again, telling her she had brought misfortune on herself and on the prince. But the girl sneaked out of the house and met the prince. When she wasn't home in the morning, the witch asked the sisters, who pretended to know nothing. The witch did up nine different types of enchanting herbs, plus salt, and tossed them into a cloth, which she wound into a ball and tossed into the air toward the river, cursing the girl, that she might be sucked into the river's current as punishment for her disobedience (overreact much?).

Just down the river the prince and the maiden were about to cross when the ball went zooming by, spooking the horse and sending the girl flying into the current, where she quickly disappeared.

The devastated prince so mourned her that he came back one year later to the spot where she had drowned. As he was crying, he heard a beautiful song. When he looked around, he saw no one. Then he spotted a yellow water lily floating on the surface of the water. And again, he heard the song, but with no one around, he was convinced that the water lily was his beloved.

The prince rode off to find her sisters, whom he told the story of the singing lily. They knew that the witch had done some magic and had hidden their sister away, but they didn't know where. So they made the prince a cake full of magical herbs and gave it to him to eat, so he could understand the birds. Then they asked him to dream and tell them what the birds said. The birds told him the water lily was, indeed, his bride. They also told him that, to rescue her, he needed to go to the edge of the water and cover himself in mud and transform into a crab, then go in and scurry as close to the water lily's roots, among the mud and reeds, as he could get. Then he must claw at the roots and hold tight to them as they came loose and ride them to the surface. He was then to follow the current and drift until they came to the base of an ash tree that grew along a bank near a large stone. He was to stop there and transform back from a crab and a lily to a man and a woman.

And so he did, and it worked. The prince and the maiden headed back to the kingdom and got married. A little while later, they were sitting in the garden when a bird told the prince to go rescue the sisters. So they headed to the cottage, where the sisters were thrilled to be reunited. One of them baked a cake full of poison and left it for the old woman, who ate it and died.

The ancient Egyptians believed the marsh was the source of all life, and this is one of the reasons that the papyrus plant (*Cyperus papyrus*) was so important to them. Most famously, *The Egyptian Book of the Dead* was written on paper made from papyrus, but it gave in many other ways: paper, boats, sails, mummy-wrap, sandals, and more were made from papyrus. Some early texts show papyrus being used to treat bone fractures and burns, and even in dentistry.

Willow

*The willow which bends to the tempest, often escapes better
than the oak which resists it.*

—Albert Schweitzer

Botanical name: *Salix* spp.

Native to: Northern hemisphere

Also called: Sallows, sallies, osiers, witch's bark, witch's rod … as there are hundreds of species of willow, these are just a few … willow, weeping willow, Babylon willow, white willow, pussy willow, black willow, gray-leaf willow, and so on.

Magical Properties: Use to help ideas, or plants, take root. Willow is useful when trying to connect with water sprits and in healing rituals.

Medicinal Properties: Analgesic, antiseptic, and anti-inflammatory, willow reduces fever, pain, and swelling. Tea can be made of the bark, and the leaves can be used as a poultice.

The Lore

Willows' arcing branches grace impressionist paintings and stretch along river-banks. They are woven into baskets and bent to form garden gates. One of the greatest genuses of plants, with over four hundred species, the willow is found in many countries, in particular those in the northern hemisphere.

I've opted to include this incredible genus in this chapter because willows adore water. The very name *Salix* comes from the Celtic *sal-lis*, meaning "near water." You will find willows prolific along riverbanks and streams.

All willows have bark that contains salicylic acid—a main ingredient synthesized today in aspirin, so it comes as no surprise that remedies such as willow bark tea have been prescribed by healers and wise men and women around the world to dull pain, including headache, toothache, and menstrual cramps.

In Nicholas Culpeper's *The Complete Herbal*, the willow's medicinal value is well detailed:

> Both the leaves, bark, and the seed, are used to stanch bleeding of wounds, and at mouth and nose, spitting of blood, and other fluxes of blood in man or woman, and to stay vomiting, and provocation thereunto, if the decoction of them in wine be drank.

It is not only a healing plant, but a plant that helps other plants thrive. In fact, willow bark contains a powerful rooting hormone that can help new plants set in the garden. You can make a simple rooting compound by soaking branches of the willow in water for two weeks. Then use this water on any new cuttings to help them establish roots. The rooting compound sold in most garden centers is a powdered form of this.

Willows can grow nearly anywhere as long as the water table is high enough, but they can even tolerate standing water. The majority of the four hundred species of willow grow throughout the northern hemisphere, including North America, Europe, and Asia.

Because of its proximity to water, frequently growing near bubbling brooks and natural springs and wells, the willow has long been considered a sacred plant, used in wands and witching rods. It is also naturally associated, especially in Ireland and Wales, as being sacred to nymphs, water sprites, and other water elementals.

Yet, this incredible plant, which can be a weeping willow, one of the most common trees depicted on gravestones, represents both a life cut short and immortality. The weeping willow grows, unlike its other more upright counterparts, with a downward arc, hence the name. Other sources suggest that the rod that beat Christ on the cross was in fact one of willow—and that the tree bends to the earth in grief and shame.

Included in Frank Rinder's 1895 collection *Old World Japan: Legends of the Land of the Gods* is the short story "The Willow of Mukochima." This story is about a widow, Ayame, who has just one adored son, Umewaki. One day Umewaki did not return from playing in the woods. Unbeknownst to his mother, he had been kidnapped, beaten, and left for dead. Although he was found by the wayside by kindly strangers, he was ultimately too weak to survive and died—"On the fifteenth day of the third month, the day sacred to the awakening of the Spring." Months later, Ayame tracked down her son's fate:

> *In the evening, when all was quiet, Ayame crept to the graveside of her child. Near it a sacred willow was planted. The slender tree moved in the wind. There was a whispered sound: the voice of Umewaki speaking softly to the mother from his place of rest. She was happy.*
>
> *Every evening, she came to listen to the sighing of the willow. Every evening, she lay down happy to have spoken to her son.*

In Algernon Blackwood's 1907 short story, "The Willows," the "sighing of the willows" takes on a decidedly more sinister tone. The story finds the main character on a canoe expedition down the Danube with one companion. In between Vienna and Budapest, he wrote, "the Danube enters a region of singular loneliness and desolation . . . and the country becomes a swamp for miles upon miles, covered by a vast sea of low willow-bushes." It does not take long, with flood water rising, for the two canoers to discover that, although they are in an area of "singular loneliness," they are also not alone. At nightfall, horrifying visions of some kind of old-world gods forming from the branches of the willow torment him. Blackwood, like his contemporary Arthur Machen, was a member of the Ghost Society and the Hermetic Order of the Golden Dawn, a secret occult society that studied metaphysics and paranormal activity, and this is evident throughout his works in reference to pagan gods of antiquity. Blackwood's willows can be heard "humming" audibly only when the winds die down. His character speaks of the sense of foreboding that the willows give him:

> But my emotion, so far as I could understand it, seemed to attach itself more particularly to the willow bushes, to these acres and acres of willows, crowding, so thickly growing there, swarming everywhere the eye could reach, pressing upon the river as though to suffocate it, standing in dense array mile after mile beneath the sky, watching, waiting, listening.

Because of his occult leanings, it is not a great leap to assume that Blackwood knew very much the sacredness of the willow and its association with ancient tree and water spirits.

The rusalki, river sprites in Russian folklore, make a home from reeds and willows. In Richard Folkard's 1884 compendium, *Plant Lore, Legends, and Lyrics*, he recounts this Czech story about a willow spirit:

> [There was a] Nymph who appeared day by day among men, but always went back to her willow by night. She married a mortal, bare him children, and lived happily with him, till at length he cut down her Willow-tree: that moment his wife died. Out of this Willow was made a cradle, which had the power of instantly lulling to sleep the babe she had left behind her; and when the babe became a child, it was able to hold converse with its dead mother by means of a pipe, cut from the twigs growing on the stump, which once had been that mother's abiding-place.

Willow has been used in basketry throughout the world. The Pomo in northern California use willow as the primary source for making baskets to carry babies. The Round Valley Pomo, in particular, use a species of willow, *Salix argyrophylla*, to make baskets, arrows, and fish-catching traps. The Pomo word for this plant is *Bäm kä-lā*. The Yokia of Round Valley (Ukiah), California, favor the *Shkä—Salix lasiolepis*. The fibrous inner bark of this large-growing willow can be used as rope or even fiber clothing. The plant is also used medicinally, including as a topical decoction for treating itches and as a tea to reduce fever and ease chills. And the coastal Kashaya Pomo use the root of the white willow, *Salix hindsiana*, to twine into baskets, and the bark or leaves to treat sore throats.

Ginny Greenteeth or Jenny Greenteeth is a water spirit who dwells in rivers and drags people in and drowns them. She tends to dwell in still waters where large accumulations of duckweed (*Lemnoideae*) conceal her from passersby. She has long arms and can reach out from quite a distance, and is especially fond of children and old people.

It seems our journey has come to an end. Thank you for lending me your company, from the castle walls of the queen's court, past the apothecary's garden, through the meadow and the woods until we have, at last, reached the sea. Let us stay here a while longer.

Index of Botanicals

The Botanist's Study: Bibliography

Ahmad, Gufran, and Abrar Ahmad Khan. "Pumpkin: Horticultural Importance and Its Roles in Various Forms; a Review." *International Journal of Horticulture & Agriculture*, 2019. *semanticscholar.org*.

Al Kury, Lina T., Zainab Taha, and Wamidh H. Talib. "Immunomodulatory and Anticancer Activities of *Hyacinthus orientalis* L.: An In Vitro and In Vivo Study." *Plants (Basel)*. March 24, 2021. *ncbi.nlm.nih.gov*.

Albala, Ken. *Beans: A History*. New York and London: Bloomsbury Academic, 2017. Kindle.

Albee, Sarah. *Poison: Deadly Deeds, Perilous Professions, and Murderous Medicines*. New York: Crown, 2017.

Andersen, Hans Christian. *Andersen's Fairy Tales*. New York: A. L. Burt Company, n.d. [This is the book I had as a child, when I was first terrorized by the mermaid's dagger-bleeding feet.]

Andersen, Hans Christian. *Hans Andersen's Fairy Tales, First Series*. Boston: Ginn and Company, 1914. Epub. *gutenberg.org*.

Andersen, Hans Christian. *Hans Andersen's Fairy Tales, Second Series*. Boston: Ginn and Company, 1915. *gutenberg.org*.

Anonymous. *Sinbad the Sailor, & Other Stories from the Arabian Nights*. Epub. Accessed Apr. 18, 2023. *gutenberg.org*.

Ayers, Peter. "Britain's Green Allies: Medicinal Plants in Wartime," from British Society for the History of Pharmacy lecture. *royalhistsoc.org*. [Ayers also has published a book with the same name.]

Baring-Gould, Sabine. *The Book of Were-Wolves*. London: Smith, Elder & Co., 1865. Kindle.

Baldwin, James. *Old Greek Stories*. New York, Chicago: American Book Company, 1895. Epub. *gutenberg.org*.

Baum, L. Frank. *Little Wizard Stories of Oz*. Chicago: Reilly & Britton, 1914. Epub. *gutenberg.org*.

Bazzett, Michael. *The Popol Vuh*. Minneapolis, MN: Milkweed, 2018.

Becker, Karl Friedrich, and Ferdinand Schmidt. *Gods and Heroes*. Chicago: A. C. McClurg & Co., 1912. Epub. *gutenberg.org*.

Benítez, Guillermo, Marco Leonti, Barbara Böck, Simon Vulfsons, and Amots Dafni. "The Rise and Fall of Mandrake in Medicine." *Journal of Ethnopharmacology 303*, 2023. *doi.org/10.1016/j.jep.2022.115874*.

Beston, Henry. *Herbs and the Earth*. Boston: David R. Godine, 1935.

Beverage World. "Beer and Henbane." Accessed Feb. 10, 2024. *beverage-world.com*.

Blackwood, Algernon. "The Willows" from *The Listener and Other Stories*. New York: A.A. Knopf, 1907. Epub. *gutenberg.org*.

Blécourt, Willem de. "Monstrous Theories: Werewolves and the Abuse of History." *Preternature: Critical and Historical Studies on the Preternatural 2*, no. 2, 2013. Accessed Feb. 2, 2024. *jstor.org*.

Boeckann, Catherine. "Planting, Growing and Harvesting Cabbage." *The Farmer's Almanac*, Feb. 9, 2024. *almanac.com*.

Boskabady, Mohammad H., Mohammad N. Shafei, Zahra Saberi, and Somayeh Amini. "Pharmacological Effects of Rosa Damascena." *Iranian Journal of Basic Medical Sciences 14*, no. 4, 2011. *ncbi.nlm.nih.gov*.

Boyles, Margaret. "5 Reasons You Should Eat Cabbage." *The Farmer's Almanac*. March 14, 2023. *almanac.com*.

Bradley, Kris. *Mrs. B's Guide to Household Witchery*. San Francisco: Red Wheel/Weiser Books, 2012.

Bremness, Lesley. *The Complete Book of Herbs*. New York: Viking Studio, 1994.

Brooke, Elisabeth. *Medicine Women*. Wheaton, IL: Quest, 1997.

Browne, Lathom G. *Reports of Trials for Murder by Poisoning*. London: Stevens & Sons, 1883. Kindle.

Burns, Jacob. "Monsters, Magic, and Monkshood." *Chicago Botanic Garden*, Oct. 30, 2016. *chicagobotanic.org*.

Caili, Fu, Shi Huan, and Li Quanhong. "A Review on Pharmacological Activities and Utilization Technologies of Pumpkin." *Plant Foods for Human Nutrition 61* (June 7, 2006): 70–77. *doi.org/10.1007/s11130-006-0016-6*.

Carroll, Lewis. *Alice's Adventures in Wonderland*. New York: Random House, 1965.

Carroll, Lewis. *Through the Looking Glass and What Alice Found There*. New York: Random House, 1965.

Cech, Richo. *Making Plant Medicine*. Williams, OR: Horizon Herbs, 2000.

Chainey, DeeDee, and Willow Winsham. *Treasury of Folklore: Seas & Rivers*. London: Batsford Books, 2021.

Chainey, DeeDee, and Willow Winsham. *Treasury of Folklore: Woodlands & Forests*. London: Batsford Books, 2021.

Chan, Yau-Ten, Ning Wang, and Yibin Feng. "The Toxicology and Detoxification of *Aconitum*: Traditional and Modern Views." *Chinese Medicine* 16 (2021): 61. *doi.org/10.1186/s13020-021-00472-9*.

Chapman Turner, Nancy. "The Ethnobotany of the Coast Salish Indians of Vancouver Island." *Economic Botany 25*, no. 1 (Jan–Mar. 1971). *jstor.org*.

Chesnut, V. K. *Plants Used by the Indians of Mendocino County, California*. Willits, CA: Mendocino County Historical Society, 1974.

Coby, Michael. *The Poison Path Herbal: Baneful Herbs, Medicinal Nightshades, and Ritual Entheogens*. Rochester, Vermont: Inner Traditions, 2021.

Collodi, Carlo, translated by Carol Della Chiesa. *The Adventures of Pinocchio*. New York: Macmillan, 1927. Epub. *gutenberg.org*.

Colum, Padraic. *The Children of Odin: The Book of Northern Myths*. New York: Macmillan, 1984. Kindle.

Coxe Stevenson, Matilda. "Ethnobotany of the Zuni Indians," in *Thirtieth Annual Report of the Bureau of American Ethnology, 1908–1909*. Bureau of American Ethnology. (1915): 31–102. Accessed Oct. 10, 2023. *repository.si.edu*.

Croker, T. Crofton. *Fairy Legends and Traditions of the South of Ireland*. Philadelphia: Lea and Blanchard, 1844. Epub. *gutenberg.org*.

Croker, T. Crofton. *Irish Fairy Legends*. Minneola, New York: Dover, 2008.

Culpeper, Nicholas. *The Complete Herbal*. London: Thomas Kelly, 1850. Epub. *gutenberg.org*.

Cunningham, Scott. *The Encyclopedia of Magical Herbs*. St. Paul, MN: Llewellyn Publications, 2008.

Dash, Mike. *Tulipomania*. New York: Three Rivers Press, 1999.

Davies, Jonathan Ceredig. *Folk-lore of West and Mid-Wales*. Berystywyth: Welsh Gazette, 1911. Epub. *gutenberg.org*.

Day, Christian. *The Witches' Book of the Dead*. New Orleans, LA: Warlock Press, 2021.

Della, Jamie. *The Book of Spells*. Berkeley, CA: Ten Speed, 2019.

Densmore, Frances. *Strength of the Earth: The Classic Guide to Ojibwe Uses of Native Plants*. St. Paul: Minnesota Historical Society Press, 2005.

DiNuzzo, Emily. "What Is Chicha Morada? A Purple Corn Drink with Health Benefits." *The Healthy*. Dec. 4, 2020. *thehealthy.com*.

Dorsey, Lillith. "Herbal Magick: Hyacinth" from *Voodoo Universe* on Patheos, March 25, 2018. *patheos.com*.

Ellacombe, Henry Nicholson. *The Plant-Lore and Garden-Craft of Shakespeare*. London: W. Satchell and Co., 1884. Epub. *gutenberg.org*.

Emerald Isle. "The Hunchback of Knockgrafton." Accessed Jan. 12, 2023. *emerald-isle.ie*.

Evans-Wentz, W. Y. *The Fairy-Faith in Celtic Countries*. London: Oxford University Press, 1911. Epub. *gutenberg.org*.

Fabre, Jean-Henri. *The Story Book of Science*. New York: The Century Co., 1917. Epub. *gutenberg.org*.

Fairfax House. "In the Name of the Rose." Accessed June 11, 2023. *fairfaxhouse .co.uk*.

Fatur, Karsten. *The Henbane Hypothesis: Viking Berserkers and Hyoscyamus Niger*. The Ethnobotanical Assembly, Issue 7. 2019. *tea-assembly.com*.

Fernie, William Thomas. *Herbal Simples Approved for Modern Uses of Cure*. Philadelphia: Boericke & Tafel, 1897. Epub. *gutenberg.org*.

Folkard, Richard. *Plant Lore, Legends, and Lyrics*. London: Sampson Low, Marston, Searle, & Rivington, 1884. Epub. *gutenberg.org*.

Foster, Steven, and Christopher Hobbs. *Western Medicinal Plants and Herbs (Peterson's Field Guides)*. Boston, MA: Houghton, 2002.

Frazer, James. *The Golden Bough: Spirts of the Wild Corn, Vol. I & II.* New York: McMillan, 1935.

Freuler, Kate. "Think of Me Tulip Spell." *Llewellyn* (blog). May 12, 2021. *llewellyn .com*.

Gerarde, John. *Herball, or Generall Historie of Plantes. 1597.* Library of Congress. loc.gov/item/44028884/.

Geniusz, Mary Siisip. *Plants Have So Much to Give Us, All We Have to Do Is Ask: Anishinaabe Botanical Teachings.* Minneapolis, MN: University of Minneapolis Press, 2015.

Gladstar, Rosemary. *Medicinal Herbs.* North Adams, MA: Storey Publishing, 2012.

Glasgow, Karla. "Sacred Datura." *Preservation Archeology Blog,* Archeology Southwest. June 21, 2017. *archaeologysouthwest.org.*

Goodrich, Jennie, Claudia Lawson, and Vana Parrish Lawson. *Kashaya Pomo Plants.* Berkeley, CA: Heyday Books, 1980.

Goodwin, Janice, and Judy Hall. "Healthy Traditions: Recipes of Our Ancestors." *National Resource Center on Native American Aging.* Accessed Mar. 1, 2024. *nrcnaa.org.*

Graves, Perceval Alfred (ed.). *The Irish Fairy Book.* London: T. Fischer, 1915. Google Book.

Gregorson, John. *Superstitions of the Highlands and Islands of Scotland.* Glasgow: Ames Maclehose and Sons, 1900. Epub. *gutenberg.org.*

Grierson, Elizabeth W. *The Scottish Fairy Book.* Philadelphia & New York: J. B. Lippincott Company, 1918. Kindle.

Grimm, Jacob, and Wilheim Grimm. *The Complete Grimm's Fairy Tales: With Intro. by Padraic Colum and Commentary by Joseph Campbell*. New York: Pantheon, 1944 & 1976.

Grimm, Jacob, and Wilheim Grimm. *Grimm's Fairy Tales*. Philadelphia: The Penn Company, 1922. Epub. *gutenberg.org*.

Groom, Gloria. *The Real Water Lilies of Giverny*. Art Institute of Chicago. Nov. 10, 2020. *artic.edu*.

Gubernatis, Angelo de. *Zoological Mythology*. London: Trubner & Co., 1872. Kindle.

Guetebier, Amber. "15 Enchanting Fairy Tale Baby Names You Haven't Thought of Yet." *Scary Mommy*. July 13, 2023. *scarymommy.com*.

Guetebier, Amber. "How to Use Straw Mulch for Vegetable Gardening." *Bob Vila*. March 4, 2024. *bobvila.com*.

Guiney, Louise Imogen. *Brownies and Bogles*. Boston: D. Lathrop, 1888. Epub. *gutenberg.org*.

Hall, Rheanna-Marie. "The Thistle: Scotland's National Flower." *National Trust for Scotland*. Accessed Jan. 2, 2024. *nts.org.uk*.

Harrison, Karen. *The Herbal Alchemist's Handbook*. San Francisco, CA: Weiser, 2011.

Hartland, Sidney Edwin. *The Science of Fairy Tales: An Inquiry into Fairy Mythology*. London: Walter Scott, 1891. Kindle.

Hawken, Paul. *The Magic of Findhorn*. New York: Harper & Row, 1975.

Hellenic Museum. "Kykeon: The Drink of Champions." Sep. 6, 2021. *hellenic.org.au*.

Hertz, Kayla. "Original Irish Jack-o-Lanterns Made of Turnips Were Truly Terrifying." *Irish Central*. Oct. 31, 2023. *irishcentral.com*.

Heuffer, Oliver Madox. *The Book of Witches.* New York: John McBride, 1908.

Higgins, Charlotte. *Greek Myths: A Retelling.* New York: Pantheon, 2021.

Hiscock, Erin Murphy. *The Green Witch's Garden.* Stoughton, MA: Adams Media, 2021.

The History and Folklore of Vampires. Ann Arbor, MI: Charles Rivers Editors, 2014. Kindle.

History.com. "How Jack O'Lanterns Originated in Irish Myth." Oct. 16, 2023. *history.com.*

Hodgson, Larry. "The Plant That May Have Driven Vikings Berserk." *The Laid Back Gardener.* April 2, 2020. *laidbackgardener.blog.*

Hoffman, David. *The Holistic Herbal.* London: Element, 2001.

Holzman, Robert S. "The Legacy of Atropos, the Fate Who Cut the Thread of Life." *Anesthesiology* (July 1998). Accessed Jan. 10, 2024. *doi .org/10.1097/00000542-199807000-00030.*

Howard, Lois Jean. "Herbs in Mythology." *Herb Society of America*, South Texas Unit. Accessed Jan. 3, 2024. *herbsociety-stu.org.*

Hulse, Ty. *A Writer's Guide to Spirit Journeys, Fairies & Witches.* Seattle, WA: Ty Hulse, 2019.

Hulse, Ty. *A Writer's Guide to the Fairies, Witches & Vampires from Fairy Tales and Lore.* Seattle, WA: Raven's Shire, 2014.

Hyde, Douglas. *Beside the Fire: A Collection of Irish-Gaelic Folk Stories.* London: David Nutt, 1910. Epub. *gutenberg.org.*

Inkwright, Fez. *Botanical Curses and Poisons: The Shadow Side of Plants.* New York: Sterling Ethos, 2021.

Jacobs, Joseph (ed.). *Celtic Fairy Tales*. London: David & Nutt, 1892. Epub. *gutenberg.org*.

Jacobs, Joseph (ed.). *English Fairy Tales*. London: David & Nutt, 1894. Epub. *gutenberg.org*.

Jacobs, Joseph. *The Fables Aesop*. London: Macmillan, 1894. Epub. *gutenberg.org*.

Jin-hai, Park. "Serving Lotus, from Flower to Seed." *The Korea Times* (Oct. 29, 2013). Accessed Jan. 3, 2024. *koreatimes.co.kr*.

Johnson, Jackie. "The Witches Garden." *Green Bay Botanical Garden* (Oct. 27, 2020). *gbbg.org*.

Johnstone, Jenny, and Annie MacDonald, "Neeps and Tatties, A Burns Night Special" *Stories of Scotland*, podcast audio, Jan. 24, 2023. *storiesofscotland.com*.

Joshi, D. C., S. K. Das, and R. K. Mukherjee. "Physical Properties of Pumpkin Seeds." *Journal of Agricultural Engineering Research 54*, no. 3 (1993). *sciencedirect.com*.

Joyce, P. W. *A Smaller Social History of Ireland*, 1906. Published online by Library Ireland. Accessed Mar. 10, 2023. *libraryireland.com*.

Karasik, Carol. *The Little Book of Maya Gods & Monsters*. Loveland, CO: Thrums Books, 2016. Kindle.

Kasarello, K., I. Köhling, A. Kosowska, K. Pucia, A. Lukasik, A. Cudnoch-Jedrzejewska, L. Paczek, U. Zielenkiewicz, and P. Zielenkiewicz. "The Anti-Inflammatory Effect of Cabbage Leaves Explained by the Influence of bol-miRNA172a on FAN Expression." *Frontiers in Pharmacology* (Mar. 24, 2022). *ncbi.nlm.nih.gov*.

Keary, Annie, and E. Keary. *Heroes of Asgard: Tales from Scandinavian Mythology*. New York: MacMillan, 1909. *gutenberg.org*.

Keightley, Thomas. *The Fairy Mythology*. London: George Bell & Sons, 1892. Epub. *gutenberg.org*.

Keister, Douglas. *Stories in Stone: A Field Guide to Cemetery Symbolism and Iconography*. Salt Lake City, UT: Gibbs Smith, 2004.

Kell, Katharine T. "The Folklore of the Daisy." *The Journal of American Folklore 69*, no. 274 (Oct.–Dec., 1956). Accessed Jan. 5, 2024. *jstor.org*.

Kirsten, Bailey. "From Assassinations to Witches' Brews: The Troubled History of the Belladonna Plant." *International Museum of Surgical Science* (May 1, 2020). *imss.org*.

Koppana, K. M. *Snake Fat and Knotted Threads: An Introduction to Finnish Traditional Healing Magic*. Loughborough, UK: Heart of Albion Press, 2003.

Kornienko, Alexander, and Antonio Evidente. "Chemistry, Biology and Medicinal Potential of Narciclasine and Its Congeners." *Chemical Reviews 108*, no. 6 (1982). Accessed Jan. 3, 2024. *doi.org/10.1021/cr078198u*.

Kúnos, Ignácz, and R. Nisbit Bain. *Turkish Fairy Tales and Folk Tales*. London: A. H. Bullen, 1901. Epub. *gutenberg.org*.

Lang, Andrew (ed.), and Leonora Blanche Alleyne. *The Fairy Books*, specifically *The Green Fairy Book* (1892), *The Yellow Fairy Book* (1894), *The Blue Fairy Book* (1889), *The Red Fairy Book* (1890), and *The Violet Fairy Book* (1901). [Today you can access these public domain books widely at libraries, in print and online. Dover has been publishing softcover editions of them since the 1960s. Andrew Lang is credited for these books, but his wife Leonora wrote most of the stories and even edited the majority of the series. Look for my *Midnight Stories* podcast episode about this topic!]

Lang, Jean. *A Book of Myths*. New York: G. P. Putnam, 1915.

Lauterjung, Isabel. "Deadly Nightshade: A Botanical Biography." *Royal College of Physicians of Edinburgh* (July 2021). Accessed Oct. 29, 2023. *rcpe.ac.uk*.

London Walking Tours. "The Hardy Tree." Accessed Feb. 23, 2024. *london-walking-tours.co.uk*.

Mabie, Hamilton Wright. *Myths That Every Child Should Know*. New York: Double Day, 1906. Epub. *gutenberg.org*.

Mac Coitir, Niall. *Ireland's Wild Plants: Myths, Legends, and Folklore*. Cork, Ireland: The Collins Press, 2016.

MacKay, Charles. *Extraordinary Popular Delusions and the Madness of Crowds*. London: Office of the National Illustrated Library, 1852. Kindle.

Mackin Roberts, Ellie. *Underworld Gods in Ancient Greek Religion*. New York: Routledge, 2020. Kindle.

The Magic and Medicine of Plants. Pleasantville, NY: Readers Digest, 1990.

Makinen, Kristi. *An Illustrated Kalavala: Myths and Legends from Finland*. Edinburgh, Scotland: Floris Books, 2020.

McAnally Jr., D. R., *Irish Wonders*. New York: Weathervane. 1888.

McCoy, Daniel. "Yggdrasil and the Well of Urd." *Norse Mythology for Smart People*. Accessed Feb. 23, 2024. *norse-mythology.org*.

McKean, Jill. "The Little White Rose." *Scottish Highland Trails*. Accessed June 11, 2023. *highlandtrails.com*.

Mead, George R. *The Ethnobotany of the California Indians*. La Grande, OR: Cat Worlds, 2003.

Meyer, Joseph E., *The Herbalist*. Self-published by the author, 1918, 1932, 1934, 1960.

Milligen, J. G. *Curiosities of Medical Experience*. London: Richard Bentley, 1839. Epub. *gutenberg.org*

Mitchell, Mandy. *Hedge Witch Book of Days*. San Francisco: Red Wheel/Weiser Books, 2014.

Mitich, Larry W. "Poison Hemlock." *Weed Technology, Vol. 12: Intriguing World of Weeds*. 1998. Accessed via University of California Dept. of Agriculture and Natural Resources archives, Feb. 11, 2024. *ucanr.edu*.

Monaghan, Patricia. *Encyclopedia of Goddesses and Heroines*. Novato, CA: New World Library, 2014. Kindle.

Mori, Scott. "Interesting Plant Stories: Queen of the Amazon." *New York Botanical Garden* (blog), Aug. 13, 2014. *nybg.org*.

Morrison, Sarah Lyddon. *The Modern Witch's Book of Symbols*. Secaucus, NJ: Citadel, 1997.

Munger, Michael. "The Secret History of Tamales Offers a Lesson in Humility." *American Institute for Economic Research (AIER)*. (January 28, 2019). *aier.org*.

Murphy-Hiscock, Arin. *The Green Witch*. Avon, MA: Adams Media, 2017.

Murray, Margaret. *The Witch Cult in Western Europe*. Oxford, England: Clarendon, 1921.

Napoli, Donna Jo. *Treasury of Greek Mythology*. Washington, DC: National Geographic Partners, 2011.

Nash, Mike. *Tulipomania: The Story of the World's Most Coveted Flower & the Extraordinary Passions It Aroused*. New York: Three Rivers Press, 2010.

National Library of Medicine. "Pomegranate." Updated August 2020. Accessed June 11, 2023. *nccih.nih.gov*.

National Park Service. "Chumash Religion: Datura." March 18, 2021. *nps.gov*.

National Records of Scotland. "Scotch Thistle." *National Records of Scotland*. Accessed June 3, 2023. *nrscotland.gov.uk*.

Nelson, Robert. *Finnish Magic*. St. Paul, MN: Llewellyn, 1999.

Newman, Joyce H. "The Truth About Foxgloves." *New York Botanical Garden*. June 11, 2014. *nybg.org*.

Nock, Judy Ann. *The Modern Witchcraft Guide to Magickal Herbs*. Avon, MA: Adams Media, 2019.

Noe, A. H. *The Witches' Dream Book and Fortune Teller*. New York: Henry J. Wehman, 1885. Digital file. Accessed via Library of Congress, August 25, 2023. *loc.gov*.

O'Connell, Rowan. "These Masked Singers Continue an Irish Christmas Tradition." *National Geographic*. Dec. 7, 2021. Accessed Dec. 12, 2023. *nationalgeographic.com*.

Ó Crualaoich, Gearóid. "Non-Sovereignty Queen Aspects of the Otherworld Female in Irish Hag Legends: The Case of Cailleach Bhéarra." *Béaloideas, Iml. 62/63. Sounds from the Supernatural: Papers Presented at the Nordic-Celtic Legend Symposium (1994/1995)*. Accessed Feb. 2, 2023. *jstor.org*.

O'Donnell, Elliot. *Book of Werwolves*. London: Methuen & Co., 1912.

O'Donnell, Elliott. *Scottish Ghost Stories*. London: Kegan Paul, Trench, Trubner & Co. Ltd., 1911. Accessed June 3, 2023. *gutenberg.org*.

O'Kon, James. *Corn, Cotton, and Chocolate: How the Maya Changed the World*. Atlanta, GA: KDP Publishing, 2017. Kindle.

O'Neill, Áine. "'The Fairy Hill Is on Fire!' (MLSIT 6071)." *Béaloideas 59* (1991). Accessed June 28, 2023. *doi.org/10.2307/20522386*.

Papp, Nóra, Dragica Purger, Szilvia Czigle, Dóra Czégényi, Szilvia Stranczinger, Mónika Tóth, Tünde Dénes, Marianna Kocsis, and Rita Filep. "The Importance of Pine Species in the Ethnomedicine of Transylvania (Romania)." *Plants 11*, no. 18 (2022). Accessed Mar. 19, 2024. *doi.org/10.3390/plants11182331*.

Paris, Harry S. et al. "First Known Image of Cucurbita in Europe, 1503–1508." *Annals of Botany 98* (2006). *ncbi.nlm.nih.gov*.

Pendell, Dale. *Pharmako/poeia*. San Francisco: Mercury House, 1995.

Perrault, Charles. *The Fairy Tales of Charles Perrault*. London: George Hathrup & Co., 1922.

Pleasant, Barbara. *Home Grown Pantry*. North Adams, MA: Storey Publishing, 2017.

Pollan, Michael. *The Botany of Desire*. New York: Random House, 2002.

Rainbolt, Dawn. "The Wee Folk of Ireland." *Wilderness Ireland*. Jan, 20, 2022. *wildernessireland.com*.

Ralston, W. R. S. *Russian Fairy Tales: A Choice Collection of Muscovite Folk-lore*. New York: Hurst & Co., 1880. Epub. *guetenberg.org*.

Readal, Maryann. "A Tiptoe Through the Tulips." Sep. 19, 2018. *The Herb Society of America. herbsocietyblog.wordpress.com*.

Richardson, Gillian. *10 Plants That Shook the World*. Richmond Hill, Ontario, Canada: Annick Press, 2013.

Rinder, Frank. *Old World Japan: Legends of the Land of the Gods*. London: George Allen, 1895. Epub. *gutenberg.org*.

Robinson, Jo. *Eating on the Wild Side*. New York: Little, Brown, 2013.

Rohde, Eleanour Sinclair. *A Garden of Herbs*. New York: Dover, 1969.

Royal Botanic Gardens: Kew. "Giant Water Lily: *Victoria amazonica*." Kew Gardens plant profile. Accessed Jan. 7, 2024. *kew.org*.

The Royal Household. "The Order of the Thistle." Published on behalf of the Royal Family on *royal.uk*. Accessed Mar. 15, 2023. *royal.uk*.

Royal, Penny C. *Herbally Yours*. Provo, UT: BiWorld, 1976.

Salmon, Enrique. *Iwigara: The Kinship of Plants and People: American Indian Ethnobotanical Traditions and Science*. Portland, OR: Timber Press, 2021.

Sarfraz, Iqra, Azhar Rasul, Farhat Jabeen, Tahira Younis, Muhammad Kashif Zahoor, Muhammad Arshad, and Muhammad Ali. "Fraxinus: A Plant with Versatile Pharmacological and Biological Activities." *Evidence-Based Complementary and Alternative Medicine* (Nov. 27, 2017). Accessed Jan. 2, 2024. *doi.org/10.1155/2017/4269868*.

Sarg, Chelsea. "Polenta, Vampires & Colonization." *The New Gastronome*. Accessed Mar. 5, 2024. *thenewgastronome.com*.

Scott, Sir Walter. "Lady of the Lake." Boston, 1883. *gutenberg.org*.

Seaweed.ie. "Use of Seaweed as Food in Ireland." Accessed Mar. 7, 2024. *seaweed.ie*.

Shade, Pam. "The Supernatural Side of Plants." *Cornell Botanic Gardens*. Oct. 8, 2022. *cornellbotanicgardens.org*.

Shen-Miller, J., P. Lindner, Y. Xie, et al. "Thermal-Stable Proteins of Fruit of Long-Living Sacred Lotus *Nelumbo nucifera* Gaertn var. China Antique." *Tropical Plant Biology* 6 (2013). Accessed Jan. 3, 2024. *doi.org/10.1007/s12042-013-9124-2*.

Sherman, Aubrey. *Vampires: The Myths, Legends, and Lore*. Avon, MA: Adams Media, 2014. Kindle.

Siegel, Matt. *The Secret History of Food*. New York: Harper Collins, 2021.

Sierocinski, Elizabeth, Felix Holzinger, and Jean-Francois Chenot. "Ivy Leaf (Hedera helix) for Acute Upper Respiratory Tract Infections: An Updated Systematic Review." *European Journal of Clinical Pharmacology* 77 (2021). *doi.org/10.1007/s00228-021-03090-4*.

Sikes, William Wirt. *British Goblins: Welsh Folk-Lore, Fairy Mythology, Legends, and Traditions.* London: Sampson Low, Marston, Searle & Rivington, 1880.

Soni, Priyanka, Anees A. Siddiqui, Jaya Dwivedi, and Vishal Soni. "Pharmacological Properties of *Datura Stramonium L.* as a Potential Medicinal Tree: An Overview." *Asian Pacific Journal of Tropical Biomedicine 2*, no. 12 (2012). Accessed Jan. 1, 2024. *doi.org/10.1016/S2221-1691(13)60014-3*.

Stewart, Amy. *The Drunken Botanist: The Plants That Create the World's Great Drinks.* Chapel Hill, NC: Algonquin, 2013.

Stewart, Amy. *Wicked Plants: The Weed That Killed Lincoln's Mother & Other Botanical Atrocities.* Chapel Hill, NC: Algonquin, 2009.

Stoker, Bram. *Dracula.* New York: Bantam, 1981.

Stoker, Bram. *Dracula.* USA: Happy Hour Books, 2023. Kindle.

Tambopata Lodge. "*Victoria amazonica*—Giant Water Lilies of the Amazon Rainforest." Feb. 26, 2020. *tambopatalodge.com*.

Teague, Gypsey Elaine. *The Witch's Guide to Wands.* San Francisco: Red Wheel/Weiser Books, 2015.

Temviriyanukul, Piya, Varittha Sritalahareuthai, Natnicha Promyos, Sirinapa Thangsiri, Kanchana Pruesapan, Wanwisa Srinuanchai, Onanong Nuchuchua, Dalad Siriwan, and Uthaiwan Suttisansanee. "The Effect of Sacred Lotus (*Nelumbo Nucifera*) and Its Mixtures on Phenolic Profiles, Antioxidant Activities, and Inhibitions of the Key Enzymes Relevant to Alzheimer's Disease." *Molecules*

25, no. 16 (2020): 3713. Accessed Mar. 19, 2024. *doi.org/10.3390/molecules25163713*.

Tepe, Emily. "A Spy, a Botanist, and a Strawberry." *University of Minnesota, Minnesota Fruit Research.* June 11, 2019. Accessed Mar. 1, 2024. *fruit.umn.edu*.

Tibbits, Charles John. *Folk-Lore and Legends: English.* London: W. W. Gibbings, 1890. Google Books.

Tregarthen, Enys. *The Piskey-Purse: Legends and Tales of North Cornwall.* London: Dartner & Co., 1905. Epub. *gutenberg.org*.

"Two Irishmen at Sea." *The Journal of American Folklore 12,* no. 46 (Jul.–Sep. 1899): 228. Accessed Oct. 15, 2023. *jstor.org*.

Ulysses, Paulino Albuquerque, Joabe Gomes Melo, Maria Franco Medeiros, Irwin Rose Menezes, Geraldo Jorge Moura, Ana Carla Asfora El-Deir, Rômulo Romeu Nóbrega Alves, Patrícia Muniz de Medeiros, Thiago Antonio de Sousa Araújo, Marcelo Alves Ramos, Rafael Ricardo Silva, Alyson Luiz Almeida, and Cecília de Fátima Castelo Almeida. "Natural Products from Ethnodirected Studies: Revisiting the Ethnobiology of the Zombie Poison." *Evidence-Based Complementary and Alternative Medicine* (2012). *doi.org/10.1155/2012/202508*.

Upham, Charles Wentworth. *Salem Witchcraft, Volumes I and II.* New York: Ungar Publishing, 1867 and 1869. Kindle.

US Department of Agriculture. "When It Comes to Red Cabbage, More Is Better." *ScienceDaily.* Accessed Mar. 3, 2024. *sciencedaily.com*.

US Department of the Army. *The Complete Guide to Edible Wild Plants.* New York: Skyhorse Publishing, 2009.

US Forest Service. "Ergot: The Psychoactive Fungus That Changed History." Accessed Feb. 15, 2024. *fs.usda.gov*.

US Forest Service. "The Powerful Solanaceae: Henbane." Accessed Dec. 10, 2023. *fs.usda.gov*.

Ventura, Varla. *Among the Mermaids: Facts, Myths, and Enchantments from the Sirens of the Sea*. San Francisco: Weiser Books, 2013.

Ventura, Varla. *Banshees, Werewolves, Vampires & Other Creatures of the Night: Facts, Fictions, and First-Hand Accounts*. San Francisco: Weiser Books, 2013.

Ventura, Varla. *Fairies, Pookas, and Changelings: A Complete Guide to the Wild and Wicked Enchanted Realm*. San Francisco: Weiser Books, 2017.

Visit Scotland. "Scotland's National Flower: 5 Facts About the Thistle." Accessed Mar. 7, 2024. *visitscotland.com*.

VKNG Jewelry. "Flowers in the Viking World and Norse Mythology." (blog) Accessed Mar. 2, 2024. *blog.vkngjewelry.com*. [Epic, gorgeous jewelry too.]

Weber, Courtney. "Using Daffodils in Magic." *Double, Toil and Resist* on Patheos. March 25, 2019. *patheos.com*.

Wells, Diana. *100 Flowers and How They Got Their Names*. Chapel Hill, NC: Algonquin, 1997.

Wilde, Lady. *Ancient Legends, Mystic Charms & Superstitions of Ireland*. New York: Sterling. 1991.

Williamson, Jenny, and Genn McMenemy. *Women of Myth*. Stoughton, MA: Adams Media, 2023.

Wilson, Charles Bundy. "Notes on Folk Medicine." *The Journal of American Folklore 21*, no. 80 (Jan.–Mar., 1908). Accessed Jan. 5, 2024. *jstor.org*.

Windling, Terri. "The Folklore of Foxgloves." June 2, 2019. *terriwindling.com*.

Withering, William. *An Account of the Foxglove*. London: M. Swinney, 1785. Epub. *gutenberg.org*.

Woods, Peter. "Hunting the Wren." Dingle Peninsula Tourism Alliance, 1997. Accessed Dec. 12, 2023. *dingle-peninsula.ie.*

Yang, Bing, Rui Guo, Ting Li, Jing Wu, Jing Zhang, Yan Liu, Qiu Wang, and Hai Kuang. "New Anti-inflammatory Withanolides from the Leaves of *Datura Metel L*." *Steroids* 87 (2014). Accessed Nov. 12, 2023. *doi.org/10.1016/j.steroids.2014.05.003.*

Yeats, William Butler. *Fairy and Folk Tales of the Irish Peasantry* New York: Walter Scott, 1890.

Zaccai, M., L. Yarmolinsky, B. Khalfin, A. Budovsky, J. Gorelick, A. Dahan, and S. Ben-Shabat. "Medicinal Properties *of Lilium candidum L.* and Its Phytochemicals." *Plants (Basel),* July 29, 2020. *ncbi.nlm.nih.gov.*

Other Recommended Resources

Dictionary and Language Library from Foras na Gaelige
Working with the New English-Irish Dictionary Project, this is an Irish translation site where you can search for a word in Irish or English. *teanglan.ie*

Google Scholar
If you're ever trying to weed out the SEO-keyword-packed madness of general internet searching, turn to Google's calmer, more civilized search engine. Try searching "plant folk medicine" or "ghost," and you can nerd out with the best of them. *scholar.google.com*

Gutenberg.org
This is basically a free library of digital books that are within the public domain in the United States, according to copyright law. The catalog is searchable by keyword or author name, and files can be downloaded in a variety of formats, including Epub. There's no subscription model for it, but a donation is always appreciated. *gutenberg.org*

JSTOR
JSTOR is one of the best resources for finding well-researched, scholarly articles on any topic, and there is an impressive catalog of folklore, magic, medicine, culture, myths, and anthropology. You can register for free and search up to one hundred articles or upgrade to a modest paid subscription for unlimited access. *jstor.org*

New World Encyclopedia
New World Encyclopedia feels like a step up from Wikipedia and is great for verifying facts you have in your head but want to make sure you're not misremembering something. *newworldencyclopedia.org*

Poetry Foundation

The Poetry Foundation is a fantastic archive of poets old and new. It's a beautiful way to expose yourself to the classics and learn about new poets. If you want to impress your friends by memorizing a poem, this is the place to start. *poetryfoundation.org*

The Ojibwe Library

The University of Minnesota's Ojibwe People's Dictionary is a database of Ojibwe language, searchable by English or Ojibwe, with audio pronunciation guides by Ojibwe native speakers. *ojibwe.lib.umn.edu*

US National Library of Congress

Head to the Library of Congress to search the archives for everything from images to books to articles to audio files. *loc.gov*

Acknowledgments

Many thanks are in order for the making of a book:

To Bill, Julie, Pixie, Hakan, Mouse, and Robin for those early years at Sloat Garden Center when we made magic in the middle of concrete. Mary, may you rest forever in a field of daylilies.

For Henrik, who always gives me the best writing advice and is growing like a weed. To KRP, for making sure I have a place to grow. To Grandma Sandy, who has a knack for making orchids bloom in winter. Thank you to Mike, Kathy, Christine, and Andrew (and Ali!) for Door County cherries and making me feel welcome at your own door. To my favorite companion plants: Olaf, Pirate Chris, and Gem. I think of you with every page and can't wait for our next adventures: musicological, botanical, archeological, and astrological. To the magical generation next: Jacob, Emma, Aspen, Aurora, Andy III, Elena, Lucy, and Lorian. To my brothers and sisters, Donn, Debbie, Wendy, Dina, and Andy, and my sister-cousin, Elizabeth, who have helped shape my worldview (and therefore this book). To Sabrina and Philly and the darling little families they are growing: I love you with all my heart. To those who committed to this family, through marriage or love, especially Ethan, Sue, and Ralph: you are braver than you know. And to my parents, Dolores and Andy, for showing me how to sow seeds and harvest plants even in the red clay ground.

Grazie mille to my San Francisco Ladies who still make time for seaside tea when I visit: Stacey, Clare, Maureen, Celeste, Julie and Cristina. Stacey, thanks for making me preschool-classroom-famous!

To Emily, Mike, and Miles: thanks for being my Minnesota family! Big thanks to the entire Bower family for being my son's second home while I wrote this (and beyond).

Thank you to Chris Hatfield for the mysterious, magical books that arrived on my doorstep at the perfect moment and for the ever-present inspiration. It's good to know you aren't alone in the world, especially when you need a horror movie date. Giovanni and Alfio, you're basically in my DNA, so no matter the distance, we're always together.

To my darling Kim Ehart, a true friend, cat-mom, and extraordinary human, I love you from head to toe. Thank you to Erin, Jacqui, and Sara O. for teaching me how to make my words go farther. And to Jen Silverstein, you know the pirate queen is next.

To my writing sisters, Mary Jane and Danielle: thanks for talking me down off the ledge and talking me up the hill. I treasure our talks and the way our words weave like vines.

A huge thanks to the members of the Writer's Well at the WBCA as well as the amazing staff, for continued support and inspiration with all things writing especially Monika, Lisa, and Libby. And to the members of the Pen and Ink Society: remember, there's no turning back now. And to Michael Kerber and Michael Pye, for believing in this book. Thanks to Christine LeBlond, Jane Hagaman, Sylvia Hopkins, Eryn Eaton, Kathryn Sky Peck, Laurie Kelly, Sam McKora, and Mike Conlon. I owe a debt of deep gratitude to Jan Johnson, Publisher Emeritus at Red Wheel/Weiser, but also mentor, writing buddy, and friend. Huge shout-out to Charles Hutchinson for an incredible, thoughtful copyedit that made this a better book. And especially thanks to Brittany Craig who designed the treasure you are holding in your hands. It exceeded my expectations, and I almost can't believe it is real. A massive thank you to the wonderful Dave Scott and the Spaced-Out Radio crew and fans for being true creatures of the night and letting me ramble on about mermaids, seances, werewolves, and occasionally gruesome fairy tales. Shout out to Dirty Fylth whose art you should buy! Kindred souls are we. And thanks to Merle, may there be many more ghost hunts in our future. Thanks to the good folks at Coast2Coast, including George Noory, Lisa Lyon, and Tom Danheiser for your support over the many years. Special shout-out to Stephanie Smith for making sure I never lose the backup number. To Jeff Belanger, for badass advice just when I need it the most. And to the incredible Joe Diamond, one of the few people who knows my secrets and helps me keep them.

In loving memory of Steve Pelto: I hope you're sketching flowers in a garden somewhere, with lots of idle time on your hands.

About the Author

Varla Ventura is the author of several books, including *Fairies, Pookas, and Change-lings: A Complete Guide to the Wild and Wicked Enchanted Realm*. A lover of all things strange, this extends into the weirdness and magic of the plant kingdom. With a deep interest in folklore and medicinal plants, she has been studying herbalism and botany for more than thirty years. Her plant knowledge comes from a combination of experimentation, formal classes in botany, and working in the horticultural industry for fifteen years. She ran a retail nursery in Portland, Oregon, as well as in San Francisco, California, and operated her own landscaping business for more than ten years. She is also the botanical brain behind *Rotten Botany*, a website dedicated to unusual plants. When not writing, she can be found wandering around the Minnesota woods and tending her poison garden.

Visit her online at *www.varlaventura.net* and *www.rottenbotany.com*.